DECK PLANNER

25 OUTSTANDING DECKS YOU CAN BUILD

Deck Designs by
Jim Bauer, A.I.A.

Project Manager
Marlin Pritchard

Written by
Scott Millard

HOME PLANNERS, INC.
TUCSON, ARIZONA

CONTENTS

Book Design by:
Design & Production Studio
Leslie N. Sinclair, Art Director
Kurt Simonson, Artist

Photographs

James Brett: Title page, 4 (top), 5, 8 (bottom), 11 (left), 12 (bottom), 15 (top, bottom left & right), 16 (right), back cover

California Redwood Association: Front cover, 6, 7 (top & bottom), 9 (top & bottom), 14 (bottom)

Michael Landis: Contents page, 3, 4 (bottom), 8 (top), 9 (middle), 10 (top, bottom left & right), 13, 14 (top), 16 (left)

Charles Mann: 11 (right)

Southern Forest Products Association: 12 (top)

Published by Home Planners, Inc.
Editorial and Corporate Offices:
   3275 W. Ina Road, Suite 110
   Tucson, Arizona 85741
Distribution Center:
   29333 Lorie Lane
   Wixom, Michigan 48393
President and Publisher: Rickard D. Bailey
Publications Manager: Cindy J. Coatsworth
Editor: Paulette Mulvin

Library of Congress Catalogue Card Number:
90-083503
ISBN softcover: 0-918894-81-6
ISBN hardcover: 0-918894-84-0

10 9 8 7 6

On the Cover:
This dramatic three-tiered redwood design offers all the exciting outdoor possibilities that any home-owner could wish for in deck livability. For more detailed information about this plan, see page 74.

Chapter 1

DECK-SIDE LIVING

What is it that makes a deck so universally appealing? At its most basic, a deck is simply an expanse of lumber. Yet a deck is more than merely a suitable outdoor surface—it is an entry to open-air living, helping make an outdoor lifestyle much more enjoyable and enhancing indoor livability. A deck is a perfect blending of indoors and outdoors—a room with the ceiling open to the sky. Because decks are crafted from wood, they appeal to the aesthetic sense— smooth and solid underfoot—a pleasant place to spend some time.

Decks have a practical side, too. They are extremely versatile, perhaps more so than any room in your home, suiting the ever-changing needs of a family. By day they can be a play area for children, or a place for adults to relax in the sun or shade. During the evening they can become a food preparation area via the barbecue, or an overflow room for an indoor party.

The unique rock garden border of this deck leads to a sunken covered area designed in brick—a good gathering or eating spot.

Multi-level decks can serve several purposes at once—with areas designated for particular functions—play, relaxation, eating, entertaining, and private getaways.

A deck is an extension of your home, and often duplicates the function of the interior room it adjoins: a breakfast nook off the kitchen; a platform and enclosure for a spa or hot tub next to the bedroom; an outdoor family room for all sorts of activities. A deck can also be a problem-solver, converting wasted back-yard space—such as a steep slope—into a highly usable living area.

Selecting a deck design is like selecting a home floor plan. It's best to take some time to determine what you want and need. In the following pages, you'll find 25 deck plans, ranging from small and simple to multi-level, complex, and dramatic. The unique feature of this book is that complete blueprint plans and materials lists are available for each of the 25 deck designs. Information on ordering these plans is located on page 102.

Scan the following photo section for ideas and project starters. Check out the deck plans offered later in the book. Whether you're only dreaming or are serious about building a deck, you'll find plenty of useful and exciting material to make your dream deck a reality.

A whirlpool spa may be one of the most popular amenities to add to a deck.

The photo gallery on the next 13 pages will give you some idea of how beautiful and practical deck-side living can be!

A panoramic view, seen from an upper-level deck, makes a dramatic backdrop for large or small gatherings.

There is no finer way to enjoy an oceanside view than from a high deck extension.

Built-in seating enhances deck convenience. Interesting deck angles add a sense of style and design to the landscape.

Incorporating trees into a deck design provides a shady place for relaxing.

With a whirlpool spa as its central focus, this deck is planned for easy maintenance and high appeal.

Casual deck entertaining comes naturally. Because this deck is nearly flush with the ground, it has been cut out to fit around rocks and vegetation.

A cozy covered deck is a charming spot for enjoying refreshments and sharing conversation.

Even a small, simple deck can complement and enhance a home.

Relive tree house fantasies—a deck attachment to a hillside home uses surrounding trees as a natural screen.

Hanging planters work well with an open trellis-work deck cover.

Decks can be built in a variety of shapes, with curves and angles to accentuate and complement amenities and landscaping.

(Left) Conversation is made easy on a cozy covered deck that acts as a gateway to a pool or spa.

(Right) A deck that attaches to a hillside home accommodates different levels with multiple tiers.

Decks can and should become outdoor extensions of their adjacent interior rooms.

Wooden decking is a practical and appealing enhancement to a backyard pool.

(Top) Decks are perfect for trellis or container gardening. The added greenery provides a sense of lushness to the plainest of outdoor areas.

(Bottom) A deck should match the design of the home. In this case, the deck extends and repeats the home's simple, sharp angles.

A wood deck echoes the rustic appeal of the home's exterior without compromising the inherent contemporary feel of the design.

A trellis-work screen with arched tops provides a measure of privacy without closing the deck area off entirely from light and cooling breezes.

On hillsides, multi-levels allow for interesting deck options and, in this case, provide a sense of "nesting in the trees."

Decks can easily accommodate slopes or irregularities in a site. Note how deck seems to "float" above the ground.

Deck space can be positioned so that a maximum number of interior rooms have access to them—even if only with a view from a second-floor window. Add table, chairs, and a big umbrella to this deck for a place to gather and entertain.

Open-weave screening used as a roof cover for a deck allows light to filter through while keeping the area cool.

If deck space is small or narrow, a simple decorative addition, like a colorful planter or two, makes a fine finishing touch.

Chapter 2

DECK-BUILDING BASICS

If the previous pages and the plans on pages 25 to 75 provide you with the inspiration to build your dream deck, this chapter contains the practical nuts and bolts to make your ideas a reality. Even if you do not plan to do all or any of the construction yourself, *being forewarned is forearmed.* Knowing the materials and techniques required to build a safe, quality deck will help you make the right decisions.

If your deck is a simple, single-level design to be built on a level site, and you have basic tools and basic carpentry skills, you might decide to build it yourself. If your site is difficult, such as a steep slope or on uneven ground, or if you're building a complex, multi-level deck that will involve extensive use of railings and stairs, it could be worth your time, and peace of mind, to seek a competent professional.

If you've selected a deck plan from Chapter 3, and feel it will work on your site, you're one big step ahead: the design is basically complete. The blueprint package available for the design will give you virtually everything needed to build the deck, including a floor plan, framing plan, building cross-section, structural details and a materials list. Further ideas and methods for customizing a deck plan to your site are discussed on pages 76 to 83. However, if you're not sure about the design and how it might work on your site, consider hiring an architect or landscape ar-chitect. He can review your plans and look for potential problems. Once the plan is settled, and all necessary permits are in hand, building your deck is a matter of following a step-by-step plan, such as the one presented here.

SELECTING A SITE

Where you build your deck depends on several factors. Often, the orientation of your home and available outdoor space narrow your options, and placement is ob-vious. If you have several sites and deck designs to choose from, spend some time thinking about its place-ment. Building a deck is similar to building a room—what will be its primary purpose? As a common rule of thumb, a deck will perform the same function as an adjoining indoor room. For example, a deck adjacent to the the kitchen becomes a place for casual meals or a barbe-cue site. A deck off the master bed-room could be used for relaxation or a sunny spot to read the Sunday morning paper. Thinking about how your family will use the deck is valuable in determining its size, shape and location.

Building permits—There are a number of practical matters to keep in mind before and during construction. Before you purchase materials or begin building, be sure you have all building permits. If your deck includes any electrical work, such as lighting on stairways, or plumbing, such as a food prepa-ration sink, you'll need permits for each of these. A bonus in having complete, well-thought-out plans such as those offered in this book is that permits are easier to obtain. (See page 105.)

Building codes—Equally im-portant is constructing the deck to meet local codes, usually imposed by city or county governments. Codes are required to be sure your deck meets minimum standards for safety and construction methods. Some of the items that are regulated (and often require permits) include the *size* of the deck, *setback* dis-tances (the distance from the prop-erty line to the deck), *railing* and *stair construction, footing depths, fastening methods, lumber grades* for certain deck components and *fence or screen height* around the deck. In addition, neighborhood and zoning regulations may exist. Check also with nearby neighbors about your plans to build. This might avoid major headaches later on.

DECK LAYOUT

Creating a *site plan* is common when developing a plan for a home landscape. It is an exercise that also works well with deck layout and placement. A site plan allows the homeowner to sketch out on paper existing features—property lines, utility lines, permanent mature plants, land contours, buildings, roads, views to preserve and views to conceal. All of this helps to fig-ure future placement of the deck,

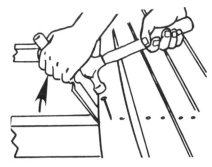

DECK TOOLS: MOST ARE BASIC
Most deck construction requires using common hand tools such as a hammer and chisel, in this instance used in combination to straighten a board with an outward bow.

landscape plants and other outdoor features. After you've recorded these, you can then note smaller, less important items. Some designers use overlays of tracing paper for different elements: one for plants, one for ground surface materials, one for built-up structures and so on. Other overlays could include utility poles and underground utility lines, neighboring buildings, driveways, walkways and even bothersome noises.

A design for comfort—*Climate,* and the many small climates in and around your lot called *microclimates,* deserve special consideration. A poorly positioned deck, climate-wise, could jeopardize your outdoor comfort, making the deck area unlivable many days of the year. Note the direction of prevailing breezes. Do you want exposure to cooling breezes, or shelter from blustery winds? Living with the sun is a similar, love-hate relationship. In cold northern climates and during certain times of the year, a sun-bathed deck is a blessing, whereas in warm southern climates, afternoon shade is almost always required during summer months. To determine shading and sun requirements, note sunrise and sunset patterns and how shade from structures and trees falls on your proposed

deck site. Be aware that sunshine and shade patterns are seasonal. The summer sun is high in the sky and shines for a longer period; thus shadow patterns are different than in winter, when the sun is lower in the sky and shines for a shorter time. Designing combination sun-shade locations for the deck for different seasons is ideal.

TOOLS CHECKLIST

Building a deck does not require a lot of specialized tools. Those required are usually found in the average handyman's garage. Gathering the tools you need before you begin construction is as important as having the building materials and lumber in sufficient sizes and quantity. If you don't want to purchase all of these, many are available at rental shops.

- Brushes and rollers to apply finishes
- Carpenter's level
- Chalk line
- Chisel
- Hammer
- Handsaw
- Line level
- Nail set
- Plumb bob
- Portable power circular saw
- Portable power drill
- Portable power jigsaw
- Shovel
- Tape measure (100 feet)
- Tool belt
- Wheelbarrow (handy to move stuff and to mix concrete)

SELECTING LUMBER

Each plan on pages 25 to 75 has available a list of the lumber and other materials required to build the deck. It will be up to you to select the wood for the substructure and the decking surface itself.

A number of wood species are used for decking. Some of the more common include: redwood, Western red cedar, Douglas fir, spruce, and a several species of

pine, including Southern yellow pine, northern pine and ponderosa pine.

Lumber is also available in different grades, depending on quality, decay resistance and strength. For example, redwood is graded as (listed from highest to lowest quality) Clear All Heart, Select Heart, Construction Heart and Merchantable Heart. The last three grades are commonly used in deck construction.

One of the primary considerations is preventing the deck support structure from decaying. For this reason, lumber that is in contact or even in close proximity to the ground must be decay-resistant. Seek out resistant species and treat lumber with a preservative before building. You might also consider using *pressure-treated* wood, available from most lumber dealers and home centers. Preservatives or fire-retardant chemicals are forced into the fibers of this lumber to protect and prolong its durability. Some precautions are required when using this wood because of the chemicals used in treating. Do not use where wood will come into direct contact with drinking water, food or animal feed. Do not use boards that have apparent residue. Wear a mask and goggles when sawing wood. Do not burn the wood—sweep up and dispose of sawdust and remainders. To be safe, check with your lumber supplier for additional precautions.

To assist with any wood selection, a reputable lumber dealer can be invaluable. He will be familiar with the lumber commonly used for decking in your area. Be sure that what you want is available locally. If you specify something that is not normally in stock in your neck of the woods, you'll pay much more to acquire it.

SITE PREPARATION

You've selected the site according to your observations and site plan, complete deck plans are in hand, you've obtained all permits and code-approved materials are gathered on site. At last, it's time to begin building. Following these important steps will help assure that construction will proceed quickly and without too many hitches.

Drainage—This is an important word to remember when beginning deck construction. Water must drain away or it will pool on structural supports, eventually rotting and weakening them. In addition, water-saturated soil beneath footings may not remain firm enough to support the deck.

The easiest way to supply drainage is to slope the ground away from home and deck so water will run off naturally. If the ground does not slope naturally, you can dig a drainage channel or channels to carry water away. Note where water runoff flows naturally and install trenches there. If runoff is not overly significant, dig trenches about 1 foot deep and line with 1 to 2 inches of gravel. If runoff is heavy, further engineering will be required, perhaps laying perforated pipe, or lining the ditches with concrete. For these kinds of efforts, it is best to consult with an architect or engineer. If possible, direct the runoff downhill into irrigation wells for trees and shrubs. This form of water-harvesting solves two problems: it takes care of excess water and supplies plants with needed moisture.

Remove weeds and turf—Decks usually shade the soil sufficiently to prevent most weed growth, but getting weeds out of the way before you begin to build makes construction easier. Hoe or pull weeds if the area is not too large. Keep cultivation shallow or weed seeds will be brought up to the soil surface to germinate. To prevent future weed growth, lay down heavy black plastic sheeting (at least 6 mils thickness). Newly

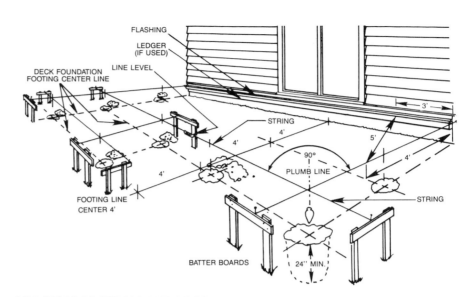

LOCATING FOOTINGS AND PIERS
Using batter boards to hold string tight and level, locate the center of all footings with a plumb line. Depth of footings depends on local codes, but at least 6 inches below frost line is recommended. Make sure the string is square by using the *3-4-5 triangle method* as shown. See text for complete explanation.

available *fabric mulch* is also a good alternative. It prevents weed growth yet allows water to pass through it and soak into the soil, resulting in less runoff downgrade. Cover sheeting or mulch with about 2 inches of pea gravel to hold them in place.

SURVEY TO OBTAIN A TRUE CORNER

A simple surveying procedure allows you to be sure your deck will be built square, with true 90-degree angles. The goal of the survey is to construct a right triangle to be sure deck corners will be built square. This is the "3-4-5 method" or the "6-8-10 method." Actually, any multiple of 3-4-5 such as 12-16-20 will work—the larger the better. See the illustration above.

The 3-4-5 method—Using stakes and string, run a line (Line One) parallel to house or wall that deck will be against. If deck is free-standing, pick any edge of the proposed deck to use as the base line. Drive a stake near the end of Line One and attach a second line (Line Two.) Run Line Two perpendicular to Line One several feet long. Use a length of string or tape measure

and measure 4 feet in length along base line. Attach another line 3 feet long or use a tape measure to measure from the stake along Line Two. Measure the distance *across* from Line Two to Line One. The corner is exactly square when this distance equals 5 feet. Adjust stakes and strings until the measurements equal the correct ratio. Use a carpenter's square in the corner to double-check your accuracy. Because the deck will be built using this as a primary reference point, it's important that the angle is correct.

INSTALLING A LEDGER

A ledger board attaches the deck to your home or other structure to give it support. However, most of the decks in the plans provided in this book are designed as free-standing, and installing a ledger is usually an option.

If your situation calls for a ledger, make sure it is attached level to its support. In most cases, the ledger will bolt to the house's floor-joist header. Attachments are usually made using lag screws or ⅜-inch thru bolts. If your home's exte-

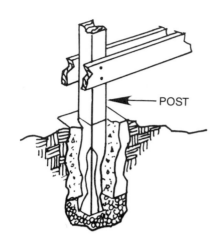

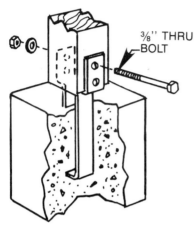

POST

3/8" THRU BOLT

ATTACHING SUPPORT POSTS TO FOOTINGS AND PIERS
Above: A *below-grade post and footing* connection. Post is set in concrete and beams are attached with nails. This is a quick and simple method, but not the strongest. Below: A *step-flange anchor* uses steel angles set in poured concrete, and post is secured with bolts and washers. This kind of method creates a strong connection that is less susceptible to wood rot.

rior is brick, expansion bolts should be used. Place bolts every 16 to 24 inches, and stagger above and below the center line of the ledger.

Use *flashing* when installing a ledger. This is aluminum or galvanized metal that serves as a sheath over the ledger. It helps prevent water from accumulating on the ledger and prevents moisture from working its way indoors.

INSTALLING FOOTINGS AND PIERS

Footings and piers create the foundation, holding the deck's support posts in place. They are placed one on top of the other. It is important to construct them correctly. Weak footings can ruin even the best-constructed deck. Local codes vary as to correct footing and pier sizes and depths. If you are in a region where the ground freezes, footings are placed a code-recommended depth below the soil level. Find out before digging.

Footing choices—Footings are formed out of concrete, either pre-cast or "pour-your-own." Wax-impregnated cardboard forms are available in cylindrical or block shapes—or you can build your own out of lumber. Pier blocks are also available pre-cast, with variations such as drift-pin connections. Local building codes will dictate which is best for particular situations.

Locate footings according to the specifications of your plan. Do not increase the distance between posts, or you could decrease the weight-bearing capacity of the deck. When digging footing holes, be certain you do not dig into underground utilities. Refer to your site plan to see if utilities are located within your deck area.

ATTACHING SUPPORT POSTS TO FOOTINGS AND PIERS

The size and number of posts are determined by the size of the deck, and the weight it will be required to support. Posts that are 4x4-size are normally suitable for an average deck. If the deck is 6 feet or more above ground, or will be required to support heavy loads, use 6x6-size posts.

There are a number of ways to attach the posts to the footing and piers. Two common methods are shown in the illustrations above. Check local codes to determine which methods are acceptible.

Metal connectors such as steel angles or straps set in poured concrete create strong connections that are less susceptible to wood rot. Drill holes in the post to match those on the steel straps, and connect with bolts and washers. All connectors should be the highest quality. Select those that are 16- to 18-gage, top-quality, double, hot-dipped galvanized steel.

Leveling post height—Height of the posts should be at least 6 inches longer to allow for variations in pier and foundation heights. The time to level them is before the final connection to the pier or footing. Double-check posts with a level to be sure they are straight as you begin to connect posts and beams. Note: If your deck will have a railing, extended posts can often be used as supports. If so, plan ahead before installing and trimming posts.

When finalizing post height, it is also a good practice to design the deck so the surface slopes gradually away from the house. A 1-inch slope for every 10 feet of deck causes water to drain away from the house, preventing problems with moisture against the foundation.

ATTACHING POSTS TO BEAMS

The illustrations on page 21 show two common methods of attaching beams, also called *stringers*, to the posts. Install these after the first row of posts has been set in place. The simplest method, "toe-nailing" the boards together with 16D nails, also makes the weakest connection. Bolting beams to posts with quality, galvanized connectors is the strongest method, and recommended. Drill the holes for the bolts into the beam, using a drill bit slightly smaller than the size of the bolt. Bolts will fit tighter this way. Use ⅜-inch bolts when connecting beams to 4x4 or 6x6 posts.

Splicing beams—If the size of the deck prevents beams from extending continuously from the first to last post, you'll be required to splice two or more beams together. For strongest connections, always splice beams together at posts. In some instances a t-strap or cleat provides needed support.

ATTACHING JOISTS TO BEAMS

Joists are attached to the beams to serve as the support for the actual decking boards. Be sure they are cut the correct size. If cut too long, they tend to bow if forced into place. Two methods of attaching are shown at right. If you decide to toenail the joist to the beam, be careful to avoid splitting the joist, which could weaken the structure. Blunting nails before pounding them into the wood helps avoid splitting the joist.

Adding blocking—*Blocking* are boards the same dimension as the joists, placed between the joists for added support. They are also called *cross-bridging*. If blocking is cut precisely to size before joists are installed, they can serve as a measure to ensure correct spacing between joists. Stagger the blocking pattern to make it easier to install.

Be sure all joists are installed at the same level. Because the actual decking goes on top of the joists, they must be the same height or the decking surface will be uneven. Check by placing a line over the joists, then pull it tight. Joists that are placed too high or too low will be above or below the line.

Splicing joists—Joists, like beams, must be spliced when they do not span an entire length. A splice should occur above a beam for support. Use a wood or metal cleat, or overlap the joist at the beam. Extend the joist 8 or more inches beyond the sides of each beam to increase the strength of the junction and to allow room for the splice.

If the joist spans over 8 feet,

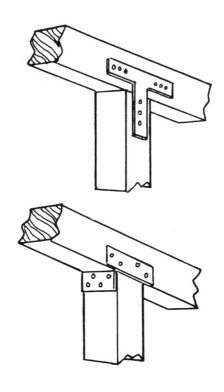

POST TO BEAM CONNECTIONS
Two methods of attaching posts to beams: a *T-strap* and *metal flange and notched beam* connection. Select a method that will be strong and long-lasting to help ensure the life and safety of your deck.

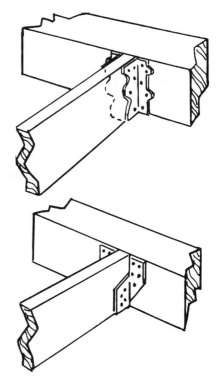

ATTACHING JOISTS TO BEAMS
Framing anchor, above, and *hurricane anchor,* below, are two common methods of attaching joists to beams. Joists become the supports for the actual decking boards. Use metal joist hangers such as these on joists located *between* beams.

apply a cross-brace to prevent twisting. The longer the distance, the more likely the joist is to twist. If decks are 8 feet or less, the end headers normally provide enough support so that cross-bracing is not required. If joists are 2x4, 2x6, or 2x8, blocking, as discussed at left, also provides support. But when using joists that are 2x10 or larger, install wood or metal cross-bracing.

STRUCTURAL BRACING

Decks that exceed four feet high from ground level require that posts be braced to resist lateral movement. Normally, bracing is required only around the deck's perimeter, but it must be continuous.

Use 2x6 lumber for all braces, and attach to posts with two bolts in each end. Use washers with bolts to help prevent gouging and result-

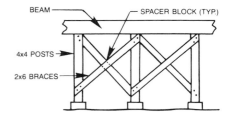

STRUCTURAL BRACING
Several designs can be used for substructure bracing, recommended for decks over four feet high. Shown is "X" bracing design.

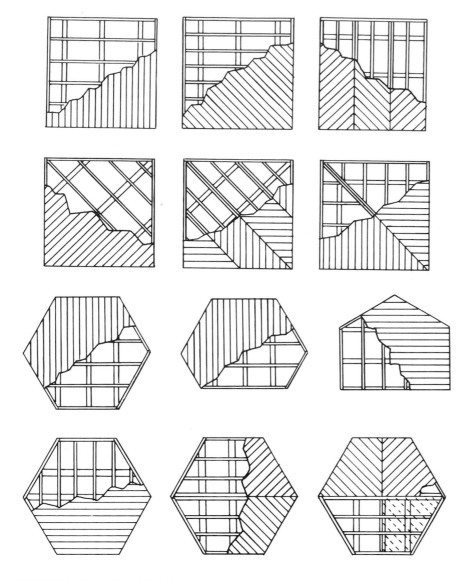

DECK SHAPES AND SURFACE PATTERNS
A selection of rectangular and octagonal framing plans shows several deck shapes and surface patterns. Note the different designs of the substructures. Select and build a substructure that will accommodate the deck surface pattern you want.

ing decay of the wood. Several methods are available for substructure bracing: single-direction, "X" bracing with block spacers, "Y," "W" and "K" designs, which refer to the outline shape of the supports. See the illustration of "X" bracing on page 21.

LAYING THE DECK SURFACE

With joists in place, it's time to lay down the deck surface: all the planning and hard work can finally take shape. You have a range of patterns in which to lay the boards. See the illustrations above for a sampling. Note that you should decide on a decking pattern before you build the support structure, because the layout of the structure could change depending on the pattern. Random-length decking, as opposed to a single uniform length or pattern, is less expensive, and creates its own interesting and appealing pattern.

When laying the decking, start at one end, squaring the first board with the header. If your deck has a ledger, leave at least ¼ to ½ inch of space between the deck and house.

As you nail boards, *measure as you go* to be sure boards are being nailed straight. If you discover you're off track, make a series of very small adjustments over several boards to make up the difference. If you try to fix the spacing on a single board, the gap between boards will be noticeable and could create a safety hazard. Note: If you are building a multi-level deck, or stairs will be attached, construct the stairway *before* nailing down decking.

A pre-determined nailing pattern will secure the decking well, reduce splitting and give the surface a more professional, finished appearance. One method, recommended by the California Redwood Association, is to use one nail to attach each board to the joist below, nailing every board at either the righthand or lefthand corner. At the next joist, if the first line was nailed in the right hand corner, nail at the lefthand corner. Continue this alternating pattern.

Some builders recommend using two nails at ends of 2x4s, three nails at ends of 2x6 or larger lumber. Always drive nails at opposite angles to prevent them from working loose. See the illustration on page 23.

Another way to prevent splitting is to drill nail holes using a bit about one-half the diameter of the nail. 10D galvanized screw nails are recommended. Blunting the end of nails with your hammer also reduces splitting.

Leave a uniform ⅛ inch of space between boards to allow for drainage. The width of a 16D nail can serve as a measuring device.

Don't trim deck boards to fit before attaching them. Allow them to overlap the edges of the outer joist. (Those locations, such as against the house where you won't be able to saw boards, would be an exception.) After boards are attached, it's a simple matter of making one long, smooth cut. See illustration at right. Be sure your extension cord will reach the entire length so you don't have to stop, which could result in an uneven trim.

RAILINGS

In most areas, decks over 3 feet high require a railing. The generally specified height of the railing is also 3 feet. Types of railings are as varied as architectural styles. Here we show only a sampling, along with basic construction methods. Railing design is important, however, because rails are a dramatic part of your deck—demanding attention. Select a design that is in harmony with your home and the deck itself.

Railings are integral to the safety of your deck, so local building codes should be reviewed carefully before beginning construction. Some general reqirements include a minimum height of 36 inches, and maximum distance of 6 to 9 inches beween railing members. In addition, lateral strength of the railing must be considered, usually designated at *15 pounds per lineal foot resistance.* But to be safe, and to meet legal requirements, check locally to be sure.

The illustrations above show the simplest methods of attaching support posts to decks, as well as methods of attaching the railings to the support posts. Plan ahead and install deck support posts that are tall enough to double as sturdy, ready-made railing supports. If this is not possible, you can bolt posts to the facing board. Either method will provide a sturdy framework.

Support posts are normally spaced about four feet apart. This can vary according to your deck and the effect you want to achieve.

STAIRS AND STEPS

Stairs and steps are extensions of deck design—allowing you to

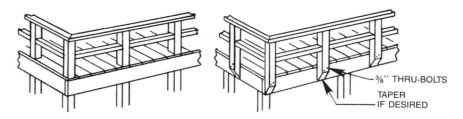

RAILING DESIGN
Left: Some deck designs allow support posts to be extended, serving as railing supports.
Right: Alternate design shows how rail posts can be bolted to facing to provide support.

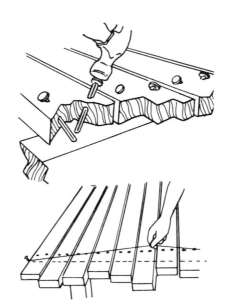

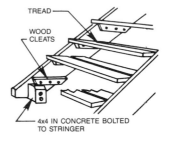

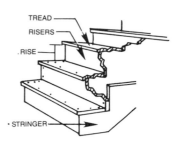

STRINGER AND TREAD OPTIONS

TIPS ON LAYING THE DECK SURFACE
Above: By driving nails at opposite angles, as shown, boards are less likely to come loose, creating a more solid surface underfoot.
Below: Rather than attempt to trim deck boards to fit before nailing them to the joists, attach boards and trim later. Use a *chalk line,* available at hardware stores and home centers, to help ensure ends are cut straight for a more professional appearance.

STANDARD TREAD-RISER RATIOS	
Tread Width	Riser Height
11''	6½''
12''	6''
13''	5½''
14''	5''
15''	4½''
16''	4''

connect decks of varying levels, or providing exits to ground level. Stairs are composed of the *tread*—the surface you walk on—and the *riser*—the vertical distance the step rises from one step to the next. Stairs are usually 4, 5 or 6 feet wide. They must be built carefully so that they have a constant *riser-to-tread* ratio. This ensures that each step is the same distance and height to avoid missteps and stumbles. A common deck ratio is 6:12, which can be built simply using two 2x6 treads and a 2x6 riser.

BASIC STEP DESIGNS
Above: With *open-riser design* steps, treads are attached to wood or metal cleats that are secured to stringers.
Below: *Closed-riser design* steps feature stringers that are notched to support tread and risers for a stronger, more finished design.

For example, if the width of the tread is 12 inches, the next step should "rise" 6 inches.

Stair *stringers*, also called the *carriage*, are the supports on which the steps are attached. Stringers are usually built from a 2x12. Steps can also be constructed as a single step from deck to ground or from one deck level to another. Some steps are constructed as a separate level, a kind of continuous step, from one deck to another. The illustration on page 23 shows the options for stringers and treads plus a chart indicating standard tread-riser ratios.

By following the steps outlined above, paying particular attention to the correct size and spacing of the support structure, you should be able to successfully build any of the single- or multi-level decks shown in this book.

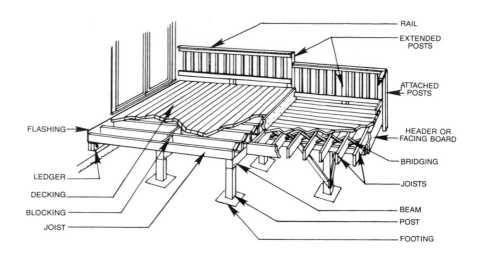

PARTS OF A DECK
Here is a basic deck structure that can be used for almost any deck. It consists of posts, beams and joists, which support the decking and railing. Also shown are additional details that make up the deck's structure. See Glossary below.

Glossary of Deck-Building Terms

Beams—Lateral support lumber members that are attached to posts. Joists rest on top of the beams.

Blocking—Boards the same dimension as the joists, placed between the joists to supply additional support.

Bracing—Part of the substructure, required when decks are four feet or more above ground. Braces are attached to posts to prevent lateral movement.

Decking—The actual deck surface. Deck boards are attached to the joists. Decking lumber is available in a number of different kinds of wood, discussed on page 18.

Flashing—Metal material that angles over the ledger board to protect it and to prevent moisture from accumulating on the ledger and against the house wall.

Footings—Supports often made of concrete that are positioned on or in the ground. Footings must rest on firm soil so the deck support system will not shift or sink.

Header—Also termed *facing board*, a length of lumber that attaches to the outside of the deck—the "facing board."

Joists—Lateral support boards that are attached to (or lay on top of) beams. Decking boards are attached to the joists.

Ledger board or **Ledger plate**—A board that is attached to the house, usually bolted to the floor joist. This allows the house to support one side of the deck.

Piers—Attached to footings, and used to support the deck posts. Often made of concrete. Posts are often attached to piers.

Posts—The upright support lumber members that are attached to piers and footings. Posts extending above level of deck can also serve as railing supports.

Riser—A term used with stair construction. The vertical distance the step rises from one step to the next. Also, the board that creates the rise.

Splicing—When the length of deck span prevents beams or joists from reaching the complete distance, *splicing* involves placing two lengths of wood together to complete the distance. It is best to splice beams at the posts for strongest connection.

Toenailing—Nailing two boards together with nails driven into boards at an angle. The fastest but least effective method of joining boards.

Tread—A term used with stair construction. Refers to the surface or surface board that is walked on.

If you are interested in more detailed information about building decks, a complete Deck Construction Details package is available from Home Planners, Inc. Composed of five oversized sheets, the package contains all the necessary data to help you construct your own deck. See page 102 for ordering information.

Chapter 3

DECK PLANS YOU CAN BUILD

A beautiful deck addition can mean so much, not only to the value of your home, but also to the enjoyment you and your family will share in using this outdoor extension. On the following pages are twenty-five decks you can actually build or have a professional contractor build for you. Complete construction blueprints are available for each of them.

Included with many of the decks are allowances for special amenities like whirlpool spas, outdoor play equipment for children, gardening areas, and other amenities. Many also include planters, barbecues, wet bars, and benches—everything needed for the perfect outdoor space. You'll also see charming deck details like a gazebo, a spiral staircase, and secluded conversation areas.

Each of the twenty-five decks shown is designed for a specific Home Planner home design for which blueprints are also available (see pages 84–96), however, all the decks are easily adaptable for almost any style or type of home. Blueprint packages include everything you or your contractor will need to complete the deck project—frontal sheet, materials list, floor plan, framing plan, deck elevations. In addition, Home Planners offers a Deck Construction Details package that provides information for building or adapting any deck.

Take a tour through our gallery of deck designs. From the simple, one-level dining extension to the elegant, elaborate entertainment deck, there's sure to be one to catch your eye. Then turn to page 102 for order information and you'll be on your way to the deck you've always wanted.

Deck Plan D100
House Plan K2774

SPLIT-LEVEL
SUN DECK

Simple in design yet versatile in function, this two-level deck provides a striking addition to a back-yard landscape where space is at a premium. Covering a total of 540 square feet, the deck can be accessed from indoors at both levels. The upper level can be reached through sliding doors at the breakfast room, making it handy to take meals outdoors. Just outside the breakfast room is plenty of space for table and chairs. A railing wraps around the triangled design, providing safety and interest.

One step down takes you to the second level. This level is accessed from indoors via the family room. A built-in bench just outside the sliding doors provides a place for seating and relaxation. The two-step, tiered design provides access to the ground level along its length.

Features at a Glance:

- Two Levels
- Built-In Bench Seating
- Easy to Build

LOWER DECK

DOWN 2 RISERS

DOWN 1 RISER

UPPER DECK

DOWN 3 RISERS

FAMILY ROOM

BREAKFAST ROOM

KITCHEN

DINING ROOM

Deck Plan D101
House Plan K2683

BI-LEVEL DECK
WITH COVERED DINING

This deck is designed for an active family, as well as for entertaining. With two levels and two accesses from indoors, each area becomes a versatile extension of its adjacent room. The total deck area adds 945 square feet of outdoor living space.

Located at the rear of this two-story, Georgian-style home, the deck's two levels extend into the back yard. Stairway exits from level one and level two allow easy access to the ground, from both the breakfast room and gathering room. Both rooms open onto the deck, for open-air enjoyment of meals, entertaining, and quiet times of relaxation. Because the gathering room is three steps down from surrounding rooms, the exit to the lower deck is made without stepping down. An overhead trellis or covered area provides a feeling of privacy and shade, making the deck's sitting area comfortable even during warm periods of the year. Built-in benches provide ample seating for guests.

Features at a Glance:

- Latticework Railing
- Covered Dining Area
- Two Built-In Benches

LOWER DECK

UPPER DECK

DOWN 2 RISERS

DOWN 3 RISERS

DOWN 5 RISERS

GATHERING ROOM   BREAKFAST ROOM   KITCHEN   PWDR   LAUNDRY   GARAGE

Deck Plan D102
House Plan K2488

FRESH-AIR CORNER DECK

This deck is designed to be built as a simple, rectangular side deck, or to wrap around the corner of a home. Depending on the home's interior layout, it could be modified to allow access from two indoor rooms, instead of one as shown here. The wrap design creates some interesting angles, which makes the deck seem much larger than its 445 square feet.

Separate areas of the deck are natural settings for different activities. For example, the corner directly in front of the dining room door is more than adequate to accommodate a table and seating for four or more people. Being close to the dining room makes this location a perfect spot for alfresco enjoyment of meals. The opposite corner, away from the dining room, is an ideal place for built-in seating, as shown on this plan. (See pages 82 and 83 for more information on building benches.) The distinct area that is created here works well for conversation, relaxation or for additional seating during meals. Steps allow for quick access to and from the ground level. Railings for safety and appearance provide the finishing touch to this simple, yet versatile deck.

Features at a Glance:

- Unique Corner Design
- L-Shaped Bench Seating
- Perfect For Smaller Lots

OPTIONAL BENCH

DOWN 4 RISERS

GATHERING RM

DINING RM

Deck Plan D 103
House Plan K2855

BACK-YARD EXTENDER DECK

This deck, though not large, allows for an array of uses. Its geometric shape adds interest in a relatively small space—654 square feet. It also permits traffic to flow to and from the kitchen—one of the most popular patterns of deck owners. It is so convenient to go from kitchen to deck-side table with a meal or snack. The plan provides for a table and chairs to be tucked into the corner just outside the breakfast room entrance. A short wall (or optional handrail) here maintains privacy and protection.

Continuous-level steps around the perimeter allow for complete access to the ground level. This kind of tiered-step design can be modified—extending the steps so the deck has several levels. Here, the two levels function as steps, and can also double as seating for casual parties. Convenient access from the covered front porch on two sides means added enjoyment of the deck from that area.

Features at a Glance:

- Completely Open To Back Yard
- Double Benches Along Covered Porch
- Appealing Angular Design

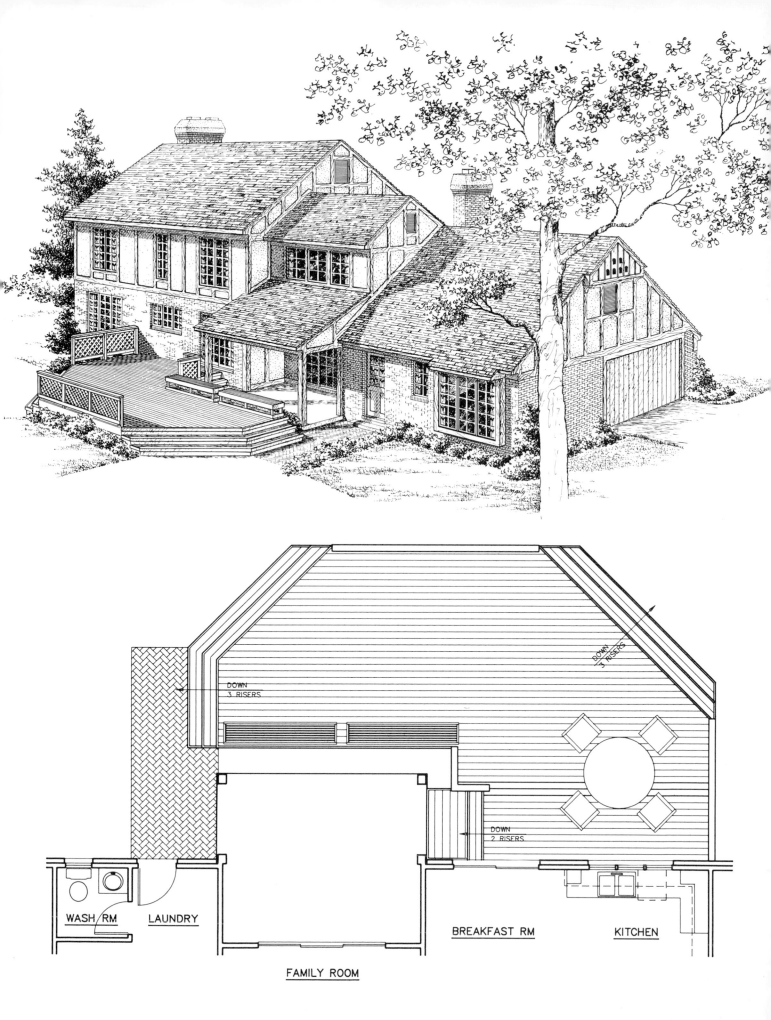

DOWN
3 RISERS

DOWN
3 RISERS

DOWN
2 RISERS

WASH RM   LAUNDRY

BREAKFAST RM   KITCHEN

FAMILY ROOM

Deck Plan D104
House Plan K2921

WRAP-AROUND FAMILY DECK

Looking for a total-living deck design? This plan, with its 1,700 square feet, wrap-around shape and multiple access, suits any occasion. When a sun room is included, this layout provides a variety of sun-to-shade conditions for almost every season.

The sun room, country kitchen and additional rooms at the rear of the home provide access to the deck. Because so many rooms open to this expansive outdoor space, the possibilities to expand indoor activities—from casual kitchen gatherings to more elaborate entertaining—are numerous. Wrapping around the kitchen and sun room, the deck spans nearly the entire rear of the house. This interesting wrap design provides practicality and privacy. For example, a quiet meal can be enjoyed near the kitchen, while children play on the built-in swing at the deck's opposite end. Three benches just outside the sun room access provide multiple seating. Beyond the benches, wide-design stairs lead to ground level. The plans allows for a selection of sun-bright or cool-shade locations. No matter what the activity or weather, this deck can accommodate.

Features at a Glance:

- Play Area For Children
- Separate Eating Area
- Three Benches To Enjoy A View

SUNROOM

LIVING ROOM

MEDIA ROOM

MASTER BEDROOM

COUNTRY KITCHEN

OPTIONAL SWING

Deck Plan D105
House Plan K2711

DRAMATIC DECK
WITH BARBECUE

There's something special about spiral stairs. They are at once whimsical and practical. In this plan, a spiral staircase is utilized outdoors as a link between a private upstairs balcony and an expansive, first-floor deck. The appearance is dramatic, plus the staircase provides upstairs occupants quick and easy access to the deck below.

This is a large deck, stretching 20 feet out from the home and extending 40 feet wide for a total of over 700 square feet. It can be accessed from the first-floor level through both the gathering room and dining room. When combined, these rooms span 31 feet. When doors are opened to the outdoors, large groups can be accommodated with ease. The deck's V design reaches an apex at its righthand side. This shape helps harbor a table and chairs. Just outside the dining room entrance, a moveable barbecue or sink combination provides handy cooking and cleanup for family meals and entertaining. Railings along the perimeter of the deck offer safety and a professional, finished appearance. Two stairways, one directly in front of the balcony, and another at the far right, allow for good ground-level access.

Features at a Glance:

- Spiral Staircase To Balcony
- Barbecue or Sink
- Dual Back-Yard Access

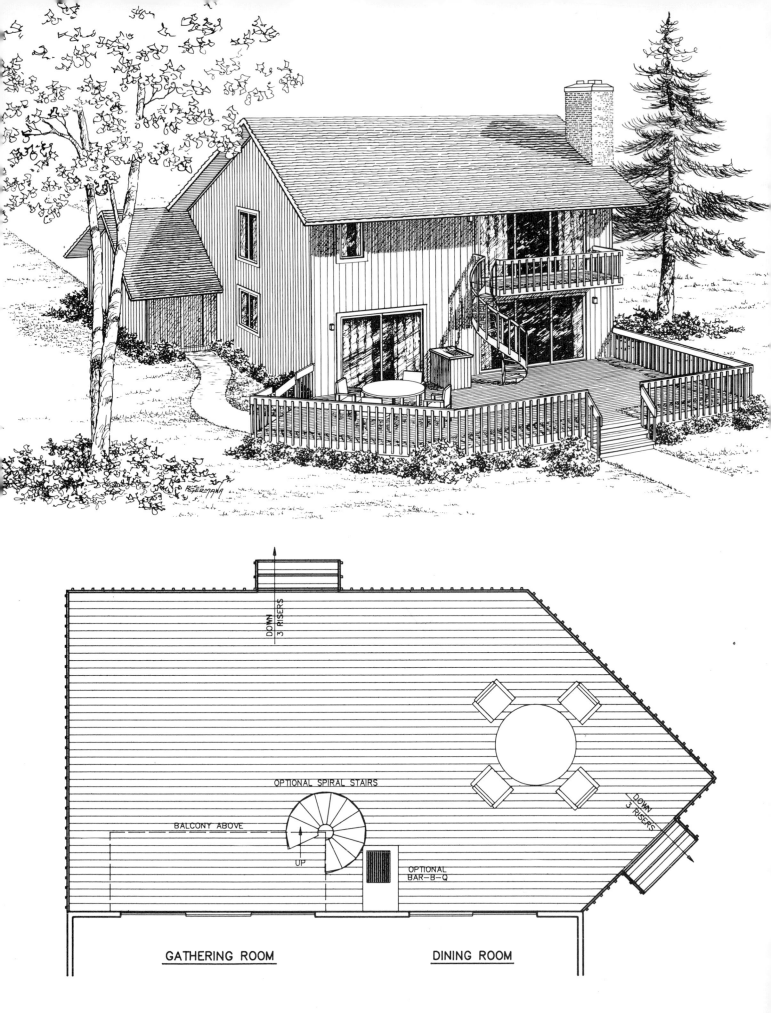

DOWN 3 RISERS

OPTIONAL SPIRAL STAIRS

BALCONY ABOVE

UP

DOWN 3 RISERS

OPTIONAL BAR-B-Q

GATHERING ROOM

DINING ROOM

Deck Plan D106
House Plan K2615

SPLIT-PLAN COUNTRY DECK

Much like a split-bedroom house plan, this is a split-deck design. One deck is more private, located outside the master bedroom. A section in the farthest corner of the master-bedroom deck is elevated to accommodate a whirlpool spa, an area that can be modified to suit manufacturer's specifications. Privacy screening repeats the same lines as this elevated section. In this instance, the screening is a simple construction of vertical boards. Built-in benches provide seating.

Two steps down to ground level, a brick walk serves as a guide to the family activities deck, accessed via the family room. The wide expanse between the two decks allows use of both simultaneously without interference between deck areas. This lower level functions as a separate outdoor room, with space for tables and chairs. A wet bar, tucked into an otherwise unusable corner, helps reduce trips indoors for refreshments—a special touch to a highly appealing design.

This 950-square-foot deck could be the perfect plan for summer-winter decking. Locate one deck in the shade, such as beneath a large tree; locate the other in a spot that will be bathed in plenty of winter sunshine. (For more information on planning for seasonal sun and shade, see page 18.)

Features at a Glance:

- Private Whirlpool Area
- Dining Deck With Wet Bar
- Convenient Built-In Seating

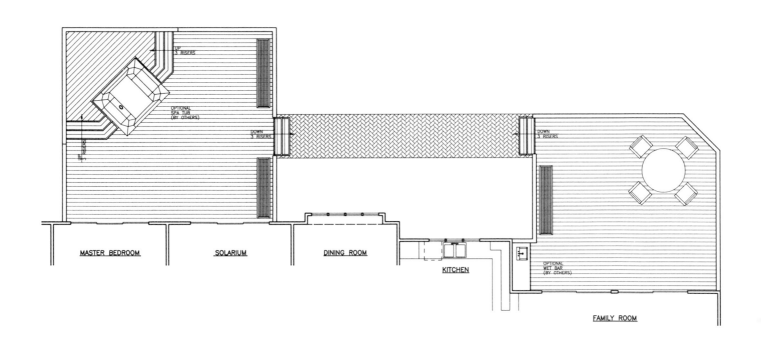

MASTER BEDROOM   SOLARIUM   DINING ROOM

OPTIONAL
SPA TUB
(BY OTHERS)

UP
RISERS

DOWN
RISERS

DOWN
RISERS

KITCHEN

OPTIONAL
WET BAR
(BY OTHERS)

FAMILY ROOM

Deck Plan D107
House Plan K2543

DECK FOR DINING AND VIEWS

This long, rectangular deck is not only spacious (over 1,100 square feet), its shape allows separate activities to go on simultaneously without interference. Relax, play, catch a meal in the sun—it can all be done on this deck. Access from indoors to out is accomplished by double doors on opposite sides of the gathering room and also from the breakfast room. This encourages the flow of traffic from indoors to outdoors—a real benefit for entertaining or for large families with various interests.

A special feature of this deck is the screening that surrounds its perimeter. This could be a valuable privacy addition for homes with small lots and nearby neighbors. Three stairways lead to ground level. Two small stairs are located at opposite ends of the deck; one large set of stairs is positioned in the center, flanked by built-in benches. This triple access to the ground level encourages family members and visitors to make use of the entire lot.

To provide plenty of space for table and chairs, one portion of the deck extends out, which also adds an interesting angle to the design. Don't miss the refreshing hot-tub area, which can be modified to fit any standard spa.

Features at a Glance:

- Back-Yard Access At Three Points
- Extends Full Width Of Home
- Multi-Use Areas

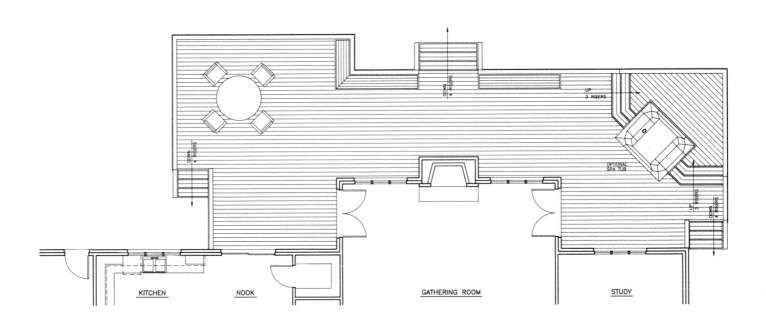

KITCHEN   NOOK   GATHERING ROOM   STUDY

Deck Plan D108
House Plan K2511

BOLD, ANGLED CORNER DECK

Dramatic—in a big way—describes this deck design. This is a multi-purpose addition that also offers some very specialized features. First, it is an excellent choice for a hillside or slope—it is elevated well above the ground level to accommodate a steep slope or a rugged, rocky surface. Second, if the building lot is flat, it is simple to add a patio below—the upper portion of the deck providing shade from above. Sun, shade and protection from the weather are available just about any time. If a lower-level patio is not desired, the area beneath the deck could be converted to a large storage area.

Because this spacious deck, with its 950 square feet of space, wraps around the entire rear of the house, it has access from the dining room, gathering room and study. The design of this deck, with its sharp angles, would lend itself well to a contemporary home or vacation home.

Sturdy railings are, of course, necessary with elevated decks. Benches in three separate areas provide adequate seating. A single stairway to ground level, located in far righthand corner, provides an exit to the ground.

Note: This deck is attached to its adjoining house with a ledger strip to make the addition more structurally sound.

Features at a Glance:

- Unique Contemporary Design
- Built-In Planters And Benches
- Private Eating Area

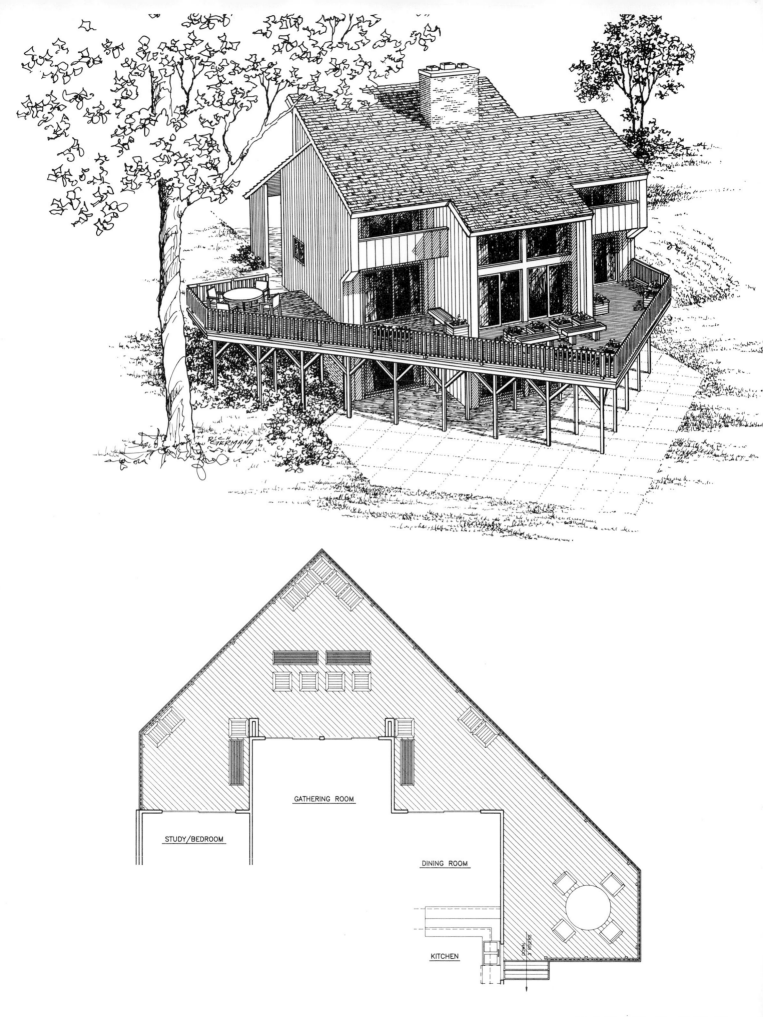

STUDY/BEDROOM

GATHERING ROOM

DINING ROOM

KITCHEN

Deck Plan D109
House Plan K2934

SPECTACULAR "RESORT-STYLE" DECK

What a spectacular deck—sure to elicit admiring oohs and aaahs from all who see it! Designed to be absolutely spacious, with over 1,400 square feet, this deck features two levels—one at upper level and the other near ground level. A railed staircase links the two levels for convenience. The second-story level with its wealth of space and built-in seating is a natural for entertaining. The ground level is designed more for privacy, featuring screening and a secluded spa.

Second story—This level is actually three connected decks, and can be reached by several rooms—all with sliding doors. Deck surface patterns change from area to area, reinforcing the feeling of multiple outdoor rooms. One rectangular deck is adjacent to the family room, kitchen and dining room. Built-in benches and planters are functional finishing touches.

Just off the living room is a square-shaped section of deck connected to the family-wing deck. It, too, has a built-in bench and planters. The stairway leading to the ground-level deck makes its connection here.

Around the corner is yet another rectangular deck, this one an extension of the master bedroom. It is smaller than the other two decks on this level, providing a more intimate setting.

Ground level—Taking the stairway down leads to the more private ground-level deck. Tall vertical boards provide screening and promote a sense of enclosure. A built-in bench provides the perfect place to relax, or to dry off after a refreshing soak in the spa. A short stairway (two steps) from this deck provides access to the ground.

Note: This deck is attached to its adjoining house with a ledger strip to make the addition more structurally sound.

Features at a Glance:

- Secluded Hot-Tub Area
- Private Areas For Eating And Relaxing
- Complete Back-Yard Entertainment Center

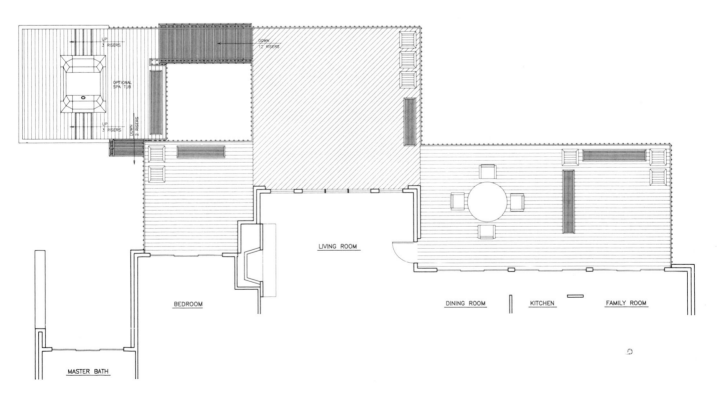

UP
3 RISERS

DOWN
12 RISERS

OPTIONAL
SPA TUB

UP
3 RISERS

DOWN
2 RISERS

BEDROOM

LIVING ROOM

MASTER BATH

DINING ROOM

KITCHEN

FAMILY ROOM

Deck Plan D110
House Plan K2969

TREND-SETTER DECK

This is an unusual design that will suit a special home and owners who have a flair for the provocative. It is particularly well-suited to homes with deep, narrow lots. The deck generates excitement from a striking, octagon shape, and by a walkway that connects it to the house.

This elevated walkway begins at a covered porch attached to the house; matching stairs on opposite sides of the walk provide access to ground level. Built-in seating is extensive—benches wrap around one entire section—covering three of the deck's eight sides.

Use this 700-square-foot design to create a totally different outdoor space separate from the home, so that stepping away from the covered porch is like stepping into another environment. The unusual shape allows for creative use of plants and trees near the deck to provide shade and seclusion. Latticework screening, as shown here around the deck perimeter, provides additional privacy and sense of enclosure.

From indoors, the covered porch is accessed by both the dining room and family room. The angles of the family room windows repeat those of the deck, balancing the design.

Features at a Glance:

- Charming Octagonal Shape
- Three-Sided Bench Seating
- Bridge From Main House

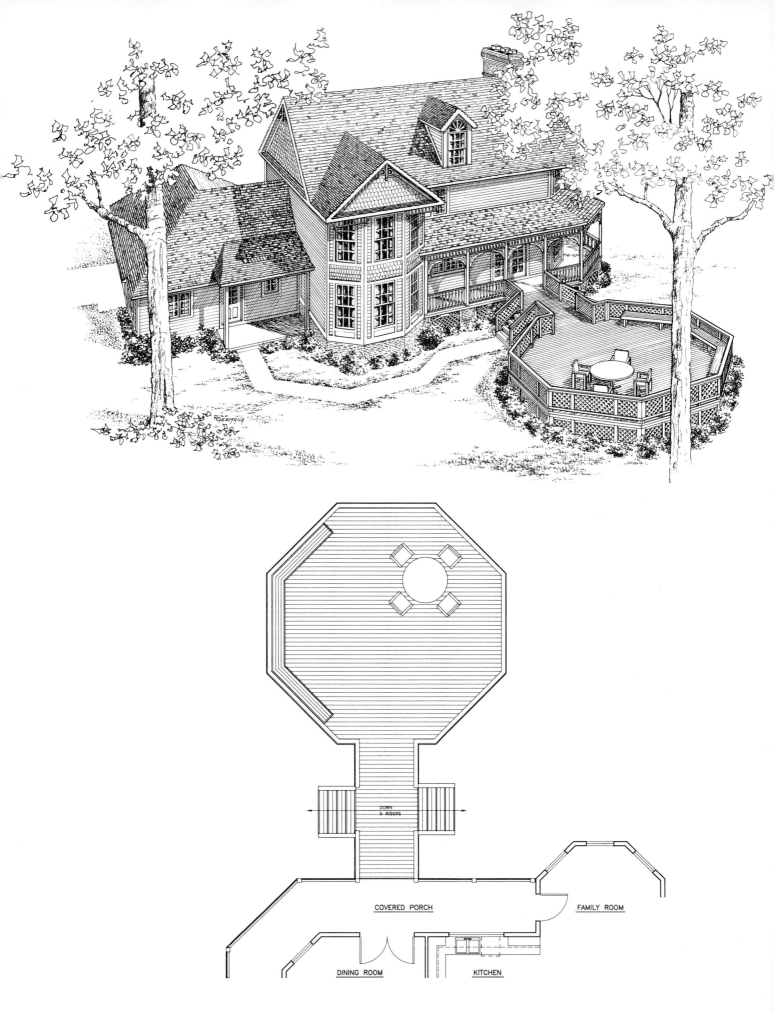

DOWN
5 RISERS

COVERED PORCH

FAMILY ROOM

DINING ROOM

KITCHEN

Deck Plan D111
House Plan K2953

TURN-OF-THE-CENTURY DECK

This creative, 19th Century-style deck is designed to provide interest and intrigue to any back-yard landscape. It is sure to draw people from indoors to out—inviting exploration of its 800 square feet of deck area and the dramatic, octagonal gazebo.

Step from either the great room or master bedroom onto a covered porch. From the porch a bridge leads to the deck itself—located only a short distance away. The bridge also serves as the vehicle for staircase exits on opposite sides. One provides access to the garage via a sidewalk; the other to the ground level.

Designed with entertaining in mind, the deck features a built-in bench that runs along the entire length of one side. The tall, peaked gazebo extends the deck outward—an interesting focal point when viewed from indoors or from the covered porch. The gazebo also provides cooling shade, and is just the right size for table and chairs.

The railing features a latticework design, repeated in the gazebo roof fascia, providing a unifying effect. A stairway located next to the bench is yet another ground-level access. A truly intriguing deck!

Features at a Glance:

- Dramatic Covered Gazebo
- Full-Length Bench Seating
- Triple Staircase Exits

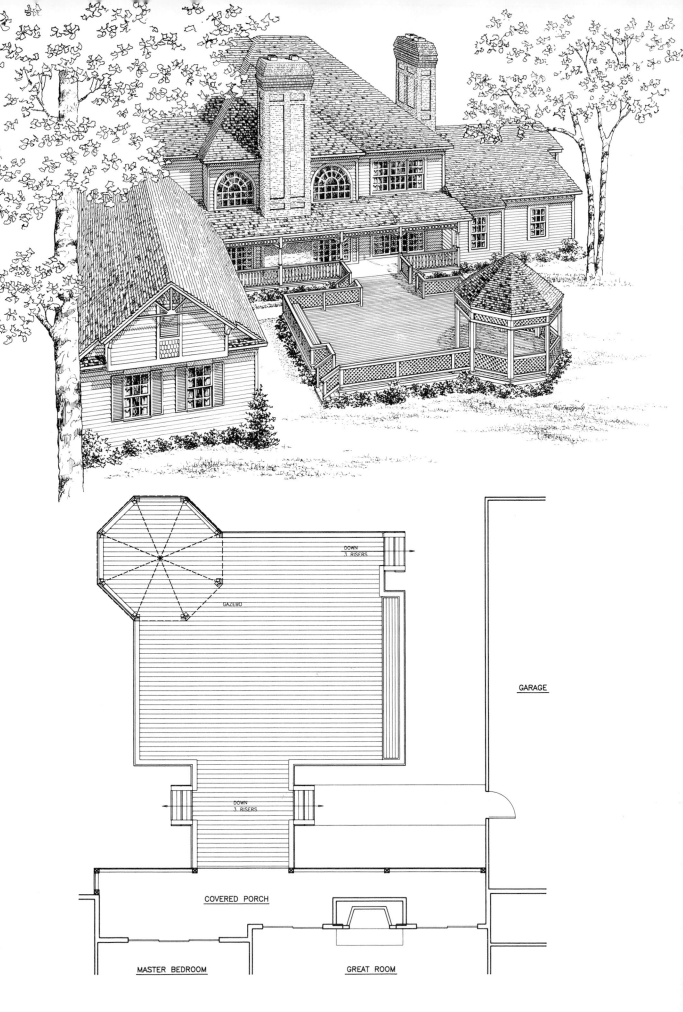

DOWN
3 RISERS

GAZEBO

GARAGE

DOWN
3 RISERS

COVERED PORCH

MASTER BEDROOM

GREAT ROOM

Deck Plan D112
House Plan K2941

WEEKEND ENTERTAINER DECK

Long and *angular* are two words that help describe this elevated, easy-to-install deck. The 750-square-foot design is contained in a single level, but the many changes in angles along the perimeter provide interest.

The deck can be reached from indoors via the dining room and the master bedroom. The deck area outside the dining room entends farther out from the house—creating a perfect spot for setting up table and chairs for open-air dining or relaxing.

Sliding doors from the master bedroom take you out onto a narrower, rectangular section of the deck, which is somewhat separate from the dining area. Benches follow the angles of the perimeter, and are protected with a railing. Two stairways—one near the dining alcove, the other across from the master bedroom doorway—provide access to the ground level.

Features at a Glance:

- Diagonal Board Pattern
- Wider Area For Dining
- House Access At Two Points

BATH

MASTER BEDROOM

GATHERING ROOM

DINING ROOM

Deck Plan D113
House Plan K2505

STRIKING "DELTA" DECK

Spanning nearly the entire width of the home, this 950-square-foot deck can be accessed from several rooms. The area off the master bedroom is the perfect location for a semiprivate gathering spot. Doors from the gathering room open onto the center of the deck. And, perhaps most convenient of all, the deck can be quickly reached from the dining room, for alfresco dining on the outdoor table and chairs.

Visually, the deck provides impact with its angular chevron or delta design— the most acute angles create an interesting scene from the gathering-room windows. Built-in benches "V" together for dramatic outdoor seating. Matching stairways on opposite sides of the benches provide dual access to ground level.

Another utilitarian feature of this deck is the garage access, near the chairs and seating corner. Moving items to and from the deck for use and storage couldn't be easier.

Features at a Glance:

- Convenient Access To Garage Storage
- V-Shaped Bench Designs
- Separate Eating And Gathering Areas

W.I.C. MASTER BEDROOM   GATHERING ROOM   DINING

DOWN 3 RISERS

DOWN 3 RISERS

DOWN 3 RISERS

GARAGE

Deck Plan D114
House Plan K2610

CENTER-VIEW DECK

Simple, yet possessing interesting design features, this center-view deck would be a valuable and functional addition to any home. Its broad, compact shape provides ample space for gatherings, meals and family activities in over 750 square feet.

The deck can be accessed from both the dining room and family room. Special features include space for bay-window pop-outs in the nook between these two rooms. The windows project onto the deck area—providing interesting angles indoors and out. A built-in bench on the deck repeats the angle of the bay window.

Access to the ground is reached via two stairways—one is located front and center, flanked by two raised planter boxes, which will help guide foot traffic to the stair entrance. Another stairway is located nearest the family room, providing quick accessibility to the adjacent mudroom. Railings surround the perimeter for safety.

Features at a Glance:

- Simple, Functional Design
- Built-In Planters And Bench Seating
- Access To Family And Dining Rooms

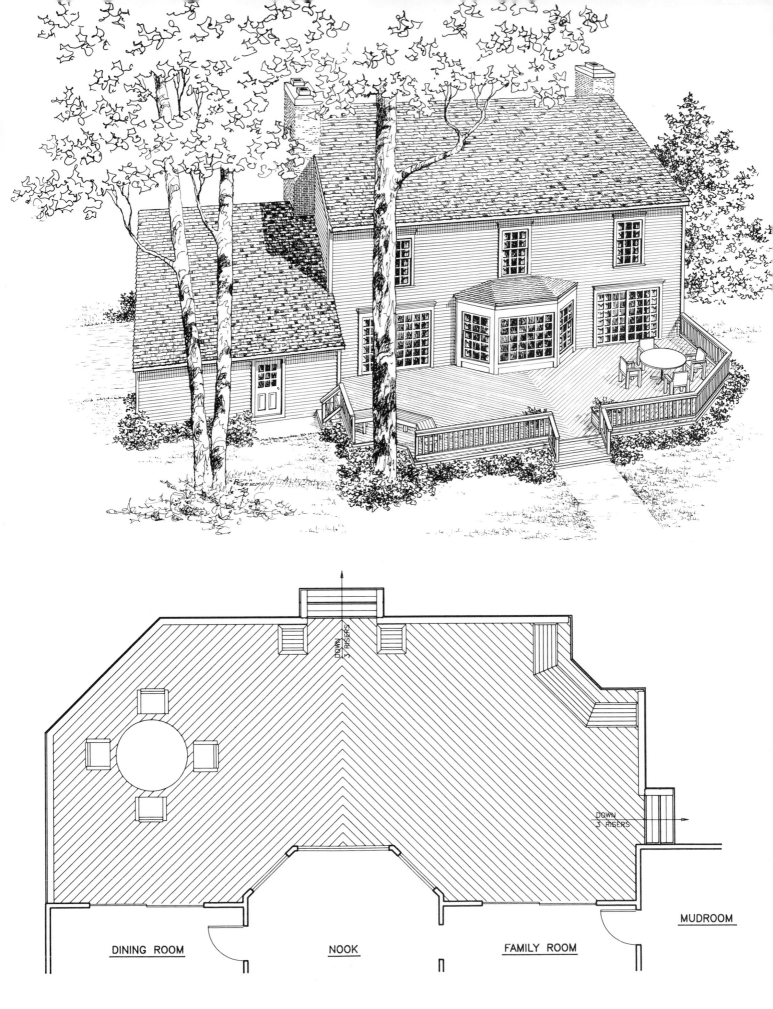

DINING ROOM   NOOK   FAMILY ROOM   MUDROOM

Deck Plan D115
House Plan K2682

KITCHEN-EXTENDER DECK

Although not a large expanse, just over 525 square feet, this stylish deck makes use of angles and strategic placement to create a sense of spaciousness and room extension. Indoors, a large country kitchen features dual sliding doors opening onto the deck, making the kitchen more accessible to the outdoors.

This design is also distinguished by its contemporary wedge shape, and could be a problem-solving design for a small or odd-shaped lot.

Built-in benches provide extensive seating—enough for fairly large gatherings. The railing is bolstered by privacy-creating latticework. One set of intricately designed stairs "V" outward to ground level, helping guide users, while providing a custom touch to this simple yet highly functional deck.

Features at a Glance:

- Interesting Wedge Shape
- Space-Expanding Design
- Room For Eating And Entertaining

DINING ROOM

COUNTRY KITCHEN

DOWN 3 RISERS

DOWN 3 RISERS

Deck Plan D116
House Plan K2826

BI-LEVEL RETREAT DECK

The broad, U-shaped design of this bi-level deck places it in the out-of-the-ordinary category. Wrapping around three rooms—study, gathering room and dining room—the 600-square-feet deck allows multiple views and access.

Another unique aspect of this deck is the creation of two separate deck spaces. One is adjacent to the gathering room and dining room; the other is just off the study. The separation of these two areas is reinforced by using distinctly different decking surface patterns. Note the angle of decking adjoining the gathering room and the dining room, which runs opposite to the decking outside of the study. Matching built-in planters located where the two patterns come together also serve to divide the two areas.

This deck also has some custom amenities to make outdoor entertaining a breeze. A wet bar is tucked into a corner created by the adjoining study and gathering room. A built-in bench is aligned with one side of the deck's perimeter, located just outside of the study.

Spacious yet intimate, the deck features plenty of room outside of the dining room for a table and chairs, providing a convenient place to relax and enjoy meals. Stairs to the ground level and a safety railing around the perimeter complete this picture-perfect design.

Features at a Glance:

- Wrap-Around Styling
- Distinct Use Areas
- Access To Three Interior Rooms

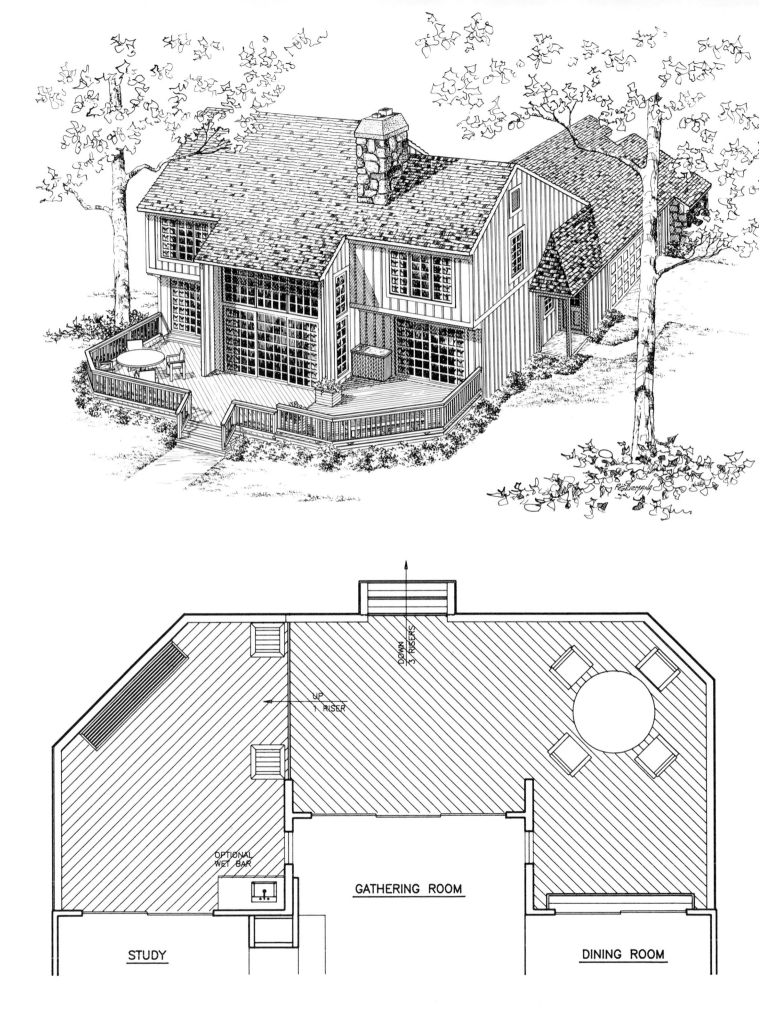

OPTIONAL
WET BAR

UP
1 RISER

DOWN
3 RISERS

GATHERING ROOM

STUDY

DINING ROOM

Deck Plan D117
House Plan K1956

SPLIT-LEVEL
ACTIVITY DECK

This split-level deck is a pleasing combination of rectangular and octogonal shapes. The result is a functional and highly attractive outdoor living space of over 625 square feet. The two-level design helps promote a two-decks-in-one feeling. In addition, each level can be accessed by separate indoor rooms.

Level one features an octagonal extension, blossoming from one corner of a rectangular section. The octagon shape is perfect for accommodating a table and chairs. Handily, this area is located just outside of the dining room and kitchen. Stairs near the center of the rectangle lead to the ground.

The second level is a single step down from level one. This area has separate access from the family room. Three built-in benches provide plenty of seating for family activities and entertaining. Permanent, square-shaped planters flank the stairs, helping identify the stairway and move traffic around it safely.

Features at a Glance:

- Octagonal Dining Extension
- Bi-Level Design
- Large Outdoor Gathering Space

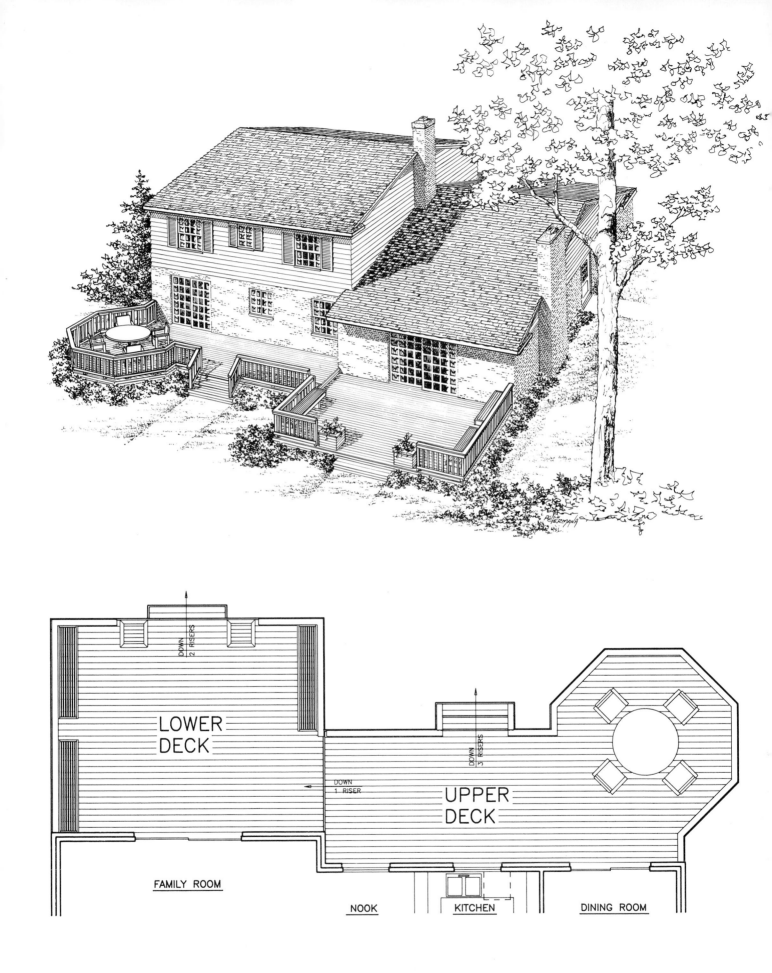

LOWER
DECK

UPPER
DECK

DOWN
2 RISERS

DOWN
3 RISERS

DOWN
1 RISER

FAMILY ROOM

NOOK

KITCHEN

DINING ROOM

Deck Plan D118
House Plan K2802

OUTDOOR LIFESTYLE DECK

This rectangular-shaped deck is long and spacious (over 800 square feet)—perfect for entertaining. In this instance, it adjoins a covered porch, a real advantage in certain regions when the weather does not cooperate.

Multiple access—from the master bedroom, gathering room and dining room—helps ensure this deck's utility. A table-and-chairs setting is positioned near the dining room to make it convenient to serve outdoor meals.

The stairway is built wide in a striking "V" design. Additional custom features include built-in benches and planters. Railings, too, surround the perimeter of the decking for safety. In this example, latticework has been added to the railing for the enhanced feeling of privacy and enclosure.

Features at a Glance:

- Long, Rectangular Plan
- Four-Point Access To Interior
- Cozy Corner Seating

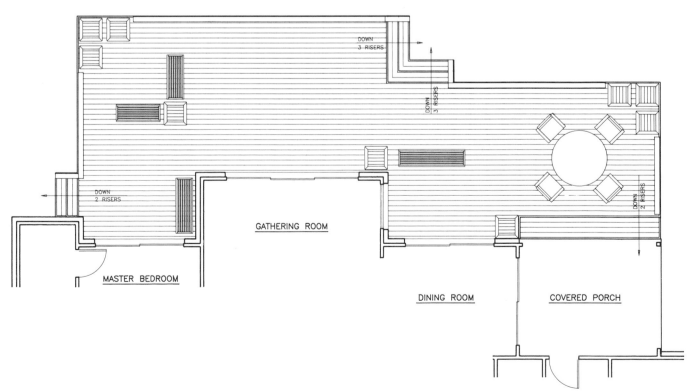

DOWN
3 RISERS

DOWN
3 RISERS

DOWN
2 RISERS

GATHERING ROOM

DOWN
2 RISERS

MASTER BEDROOM

DINING ROOM

COVERED PORCH

Deck Plan D119
House Plan K2356

TRI-LEVEL DECK WITH GRILL

This deck offers the best of both worlds. With three levels totaling over 650 square feet and an elongated shape, it is well-suited for simultaneous activities without disturbing the participating parties. Because the deck areas are linked and easy to reach, it is also excellent for large gatherings. Stairways are not required to go from one level to the next: The deck is thoughtfully designed so that each level has a change in elevation equal to a step. The result is a deck composed of three separate areas, made even more distinctive by contrasting surface patterns for each area. In fact, each section could be built separately, beginning with the upper section.

The geometric angles of the deck's perimeter add interest, and provide the opportunity for some unique features, such as the large, three-sided bench that wraps around one extended deck section.

Looking for convenience? A few steps out the kitchen door there's room for table and chairs—a relaxing place for fresh-air meals. Looking for versatility? The octagonal deck design effectively extends the livability of the covered porch, which can be reached from the family room. What's more, with garage access next to the covered porch, transportation of furniture to and from the deck is made simple.

In addition to the expansive bench seating, a moveable grill is installed near the kitchen door for barbecues. The grill can also be built as a wet bar. Planters add a finishing touch. Access to the ground level is via two exits: one near the kitchen, the other outside the covered porch.

Features at a Glance:

- Three Lovely Levels
- Outdoor Barbecue Grill
- Quaint Conversation Area

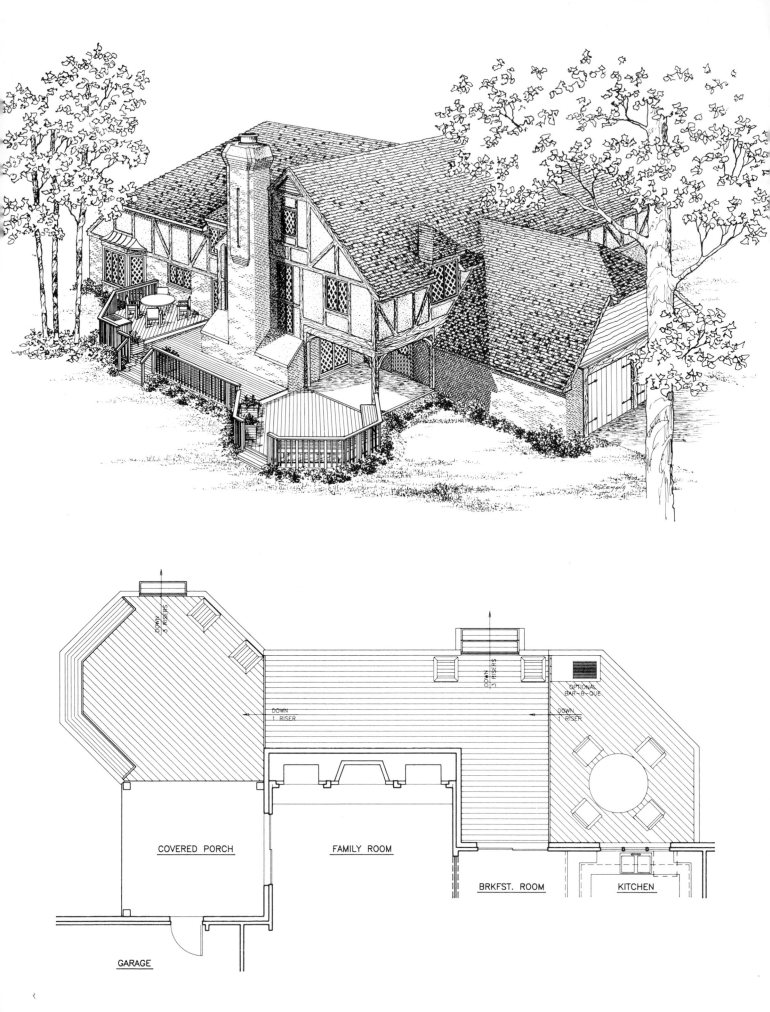

COVERED PORCH

FAMILY ROOM

BRKFST. ROOM

KITCHEN

GARAGE

DOWN 3 RISERS

DOWN 3 RISERS

DOWN 1 RISER

DOWN 1 RISER

OPTIONAL BAR-B-QUE

Deck Plan D120
House Plan K2379

CONTEMPORARY LEISURE DECK

A contemporary design is just one attribute of this diminutive yet appealing deck. An overall feeling of spaciousness is achieved in a small area (550 square feet) due to the creative changes in angle and space. This design would work extremely well in an odd-shaped lot, or where existing trees or other landscape features require some ingenuity and imagination to achieve a good "fit."

Benches are built in between matching planters in an area outside of the living room for an intimate seating arrangement. The deck extends outward dramatically to create a large area outside of the family room, with plenty of space for table and chairs. Railing surrounds the deck for a finishing touch, as well as for safety. A simple, single step down provides access to ground level in three different corners of the deck.

Features at a Glance:

- Avant-Garde Styling
- Casual Outdoor Dining
- Three Exits To Back Yard

DOWN
2 RISERS

DOWN
2 RISERS

DOWN
2 RISERS

LIVING ROOM

FAMILY ROOM

DINING ROOM

Deck Plan D121
House Plan K2781

ANGULAR WINGED DECK

This is an exciting, symmetrical deck of over 1,500 square feet that invites exploration—extending from the home in a dramatic fashion. It is a perfect deck for a site blessed with a view—the deck angles command the eye out and away toward the horizon.

Three levels and three accesses—from the study, gathering room and master bedroom—make this a highly versatile and usable deck. It can be utilized as three private decks, or one, extremely spacious deck. The centered, V-shaped section, reached by twin sliding doors from the gathering room, is on a level two steps down from smaller, matching decks on opposite sides. The deck surface pattern is laid in a V pointing outward, reinforcing the engaging, geometric design. The deck can be built in stages, beginning with the center section and later adding the wings.

Three exits to the ground level make it easy to move about the back yard. Built-in benches flank each exit; planters at selected corners add the finishing touches to a truly fine deck design.

Features at a Glance:

- Unusual Swept-Wing Design
- Sunken Entertaining Deck
- Private Master Bedroom And Study Extensions

STUDY

GATHERING ROOM

MASTER BEDROOM

Deck Plan D122
House Plan K2850

DECK FOR A SPLIT-LEVEL HOME

The split-level design of this deck is the perfect complement to the split-level house plan, and even enhances its dramatic style. With a square footage of over 1,100, it allows two activities to go on simultaneously in almost complete privacy because the deck areas are that separate and distinct.

The main deck level can be reached by twin sliding doors from the family room or from an additional set of sliding doors in the breakfast room. The spacious, rectangular shape of this level provides ample room for activities. A table and chairs fit nicely into a corner directly across from the breakfast room entrance. Nearby, a stairway leads to the ground. Outside the family room, an extensive, L-shaped, built-in bench provides lots of seating. A low, dividing screen repeats the L-shape of the bench to separate the two deck areas.

A railed stairway with seven steps takes you to the second deck, which can also be reached from the teenage activities room. In some house plans, this deck area could serve as a lower-level bedroom wing. Here the kids can enjoy get-togethers, homework or plain old relaxing without bothering the neighboring deck upstairs. Built-in planters and a pair of benches help make this deck cozy. Access to ground level is simple with two exits—one near the stairway to the main deck; the second heading toward a side yard.

Features at a Glance:

- Split-Level Plan
- Latticework Screens
- Separate Living And Activities Decks

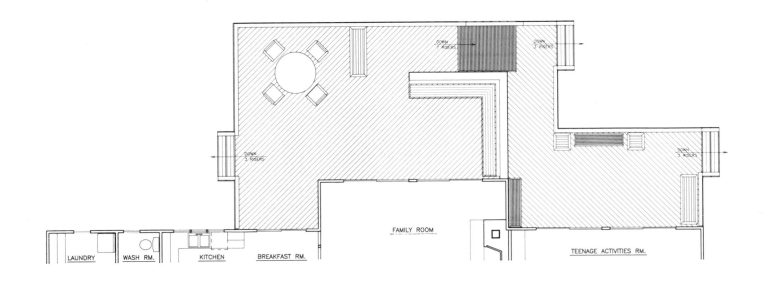

LAUNDRY   WASH RM.   KITCHEN   BREAKFAST RM.   FAMILY ROOM   TEENAGE ACTIVITIES RM.

Deck Plan D123
House Plan K2949

GRACIOUS GARDEN DECK

This is a deck of many surprises, all of which are artfully integrated into its design. A delightful, deck-level garden area, a private space off the master bedroom, and a unique treatment of moveable planters combined with ground exits are highlights.

The deck wraps around most of the rear of this home and encompasses over 850 square feet. The largest portion is accessed from the gathering room and dining room via three sets of sliding doors. There's plenty of space for table and chairs just outside the dining room. The deck sits on the ground level, so steps are not required to reach the back yard. Built-in planters are set at right angles to the two ground exits, giving the deck's perimeter an interesting, jagged shape.

The garden area is an open space in the deck; the garden is planted directly in the ground just below. This is a simple design but highly effective: the garden can be viewed from the gathering room, and watering and planting is performed from the deck. Benches surround the garden area, providing seating and safety.

Tucked around the corner, a small, intimate area adjoins the master bedroom. An exit to the ground is provided here as well.

Features at a Glance:

- Abundant Built-In Gardening Planters
- Interesting, Angled Eating Space
- Private Master Suite Deck

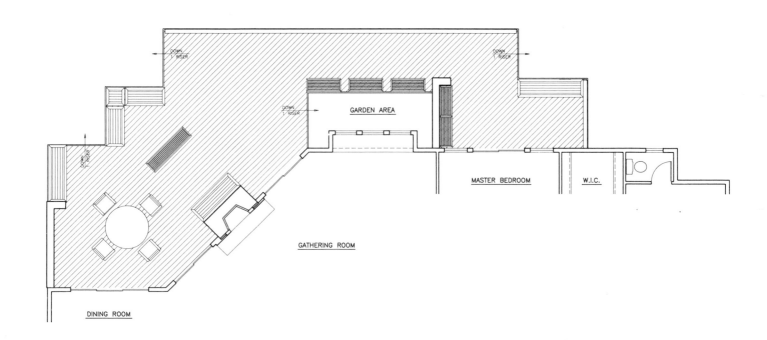

DOWN 1 RISER

DOWN 1 RISER

DOWN 1 RISER

GARDEN AREA

MASTER BEDROOM

W.I.C.

DOWN 1 RISER

GATHERING ROOM

DINING ROOM

Deck Plan D124
House Plan K2913

TERRACED DECK FOR ENTERTAINING

This spacious, terraced deck encompasses over 1,600 square feet and features three levels flowing quite naturally from one to another. The shapes and levels have a dual purpose: Each level could easily accommodate a small get-together. Or, when entertaining, large groups of people can overflow to the different levels, creating a variety of outdoor spaces for separate conversations.

Entrance to the deck can be made from the breakfast room, dining room, a family bedroom and master bedroom. A matching pair of built-in benches flank the deck at opposite sides near the breakfast room and master bedroom entrances. Gathering-room windows on opposite sides of the fireplace provide dramatic views of the deck where the steps link one level to another.

Table and chairs are set into a V-shaped nook directly in front of the dining room, and near the stairs that take you to the lower-level deck. Stairs on the lowest level provide a central exit to the back yard.

Plan D124 is featured on the cover of this book.

Features at a Glance:

- Three Distinct Levels
- Dramatic Use Of Angles And Overlooks
- Featured Cover Deck

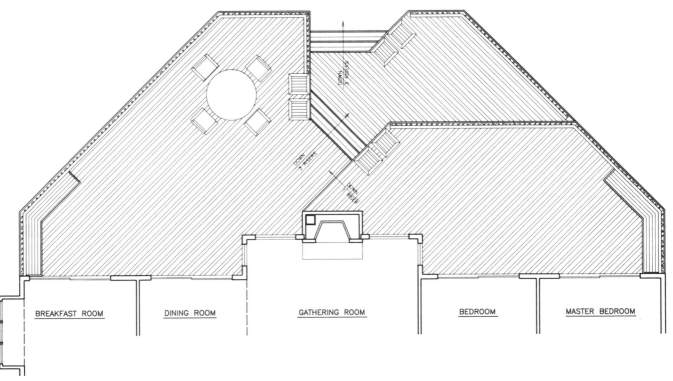

BREAKFAST ROOM   DINING ROOM   GATHERING ROOM   BEDROOM   MASTER BEDROOM

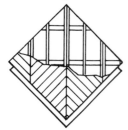

Chapter 4

ADAPTING THE DECK PLANS TO YOUR HOME AND SITE

You've studied the deck plans in Chapter 3, pages 25 to 75, and discovered a design you like. The plan suits your home and property, but you know some adjustments must be made to make the deck right for you and your family. Perhaps access to the interior of your home is different than what is shown on the plan. Or it could be that the deck is too wide, or too small. Or your fireplace juts into the area and the deck must wrap around it. Or you love a particular single-level design, but have your heart set on a multi-level deck.

Don't despair. In many circumstances, modifications to our deck plans will be required. These changes, much like modifications to an architectural plan, are not difficult to accomplish, as long as you take your time and *plan ahead*.

Planning ahead means being sure that changes to a design, particularly the framing plan, are done properly so the deck is built strong and safe. It is especially important that the correct number of support posts and beams are incorporated into the new size and shape of your deck.

The blueprint package, available separately for each plan in this book, provides detailed information on how to build the deck: a framing plan, a floor plan, separate elevations for left, right and front views, as well as cross-section details of how to construct footings, and how to connect beams to joists—right down to the size and placement of each bolt and nail. Information on how to customize these deck plans to your situation is presented in the following pages.

The Deck Construction Details package, available separately, (see page 102), discusses and illustrates many variations of deck construction. This package could be helpful if you are going to do any major modifications to one of the deck plans. Also included are charts that show how to select proper lumber sizes and span distances for your deck.

If you are creating your own working drawings based on the plans in this book, you'll need to develop your own framing plan and other details. The following pages provide guidelines on how to do this, as well as adjusting the deck plans in this book to suit your site.

If you don't feel confident making more than minor changes to a plan, it is best to seek the advice of a local architect or builder.

He can adapt a plan to suit your individual needs. He'll also make sure the deck is safe and conforms to required building codes. Keep in mind, too, that making modifications to an existing plan will be much less expensive than having an architect develop one from scratch.

Even if you order the working drawings from this book and make changes—or if you create your own working drawings from basic plans shown in this book—we recommend that you seek the help of a qualified architect or engineer to double-check your work. You will also want to check with local building officials to make certain your new deck plans conform to local codes.

SOME ADAPTATION GUIDELINES

As mentioned, most deck plans will require some adjustments, often minor, before they can be built on your lot. Before proceeding with major changes, try sketching a prospective design on paper. Or use other means to visualize a deck, such as outlining its perimeter with stakes and string, or even garden hose, on the proposed site. Seeing the actual space the deck will require before beginning modifications can reveal problems or bring additional changes to mind.

Maintain substructure strength—To be sure the deck is built safely, use the same sizes and spacing of substructure lumber throughout your modifications as shown in the basic framing plan. This includes uniform size and spacing of posts, beams, and joists. All should be designated on your deck framing plan.

In general, follow the recommended maximum spacing and recommended minimum lumber size. See charts, page 79. This will allow you to expand a deck in almost any direction without jeopardizing its structural stability.

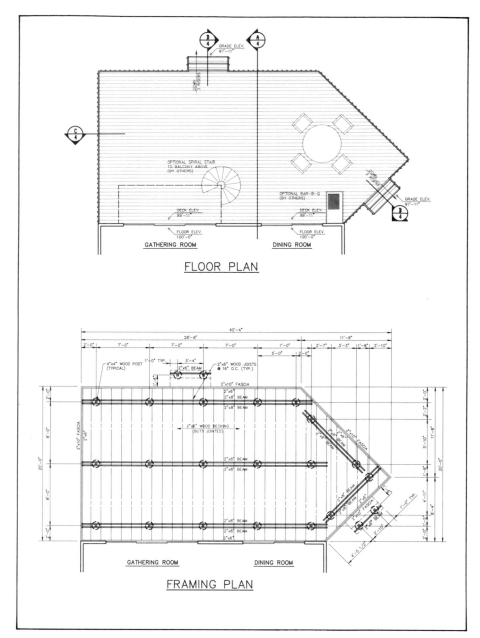

FLOOR PLAN

FRAMING PLAN

Working around existing landscaping—One of the nice features of a deck is that it is easily adaptable, and can often be molded around existing trees and shrubs in the landscape. These valuable plants provide shade and privacy around a deck, and should remain part of the scheme, if possible. In the right setting, a tree growing up through a deck can be quite dramatic.

Keep two points in mind if dealing with a tree near or protruding through the structure of a deck: Do not attach the deck to a tree. Both the deck and the tree will be damaged when the tree moves in the wind or expands due to growth. Also, provide plenty of space around the tree trunk to allow the tree adequate movement in the wind and room for trunk growth.

STAND-ALONE DESIGNS

Many of the deck plans in this book, shown on pages 25 to 75, are designed to be constructed as *stand-alone decks*. This means the deck is not connected to the house foundation or siding. It is supported by its

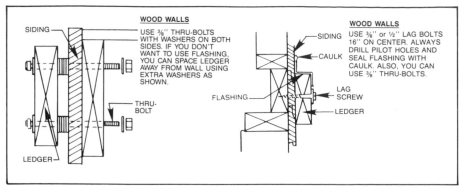

ADDING A LEDGER
Above are two methods of attaching a ledger to wood walls.

own foundation, posts and beams. This kind of design could be a tremendous benefit if the deck or your home should shift or settle slightly after construction. Settling can force the deck to buckle and shear, causing damage to structural supports. A stand-alone, self-supporting deck does not place stress on the home, nor does it become stressed.

All plans in this book are formulated so that decks can be modified to fit almost any style of home or outside wall configuration. This is due to the fact that each plan is designed so the first two support posts are located at least two feet from the house foundation. This is done to make it easier for the deck to be custom-cut around odd shapes or offsets. Examples of these would be a bay window or a fireplace that projects into the deck area. Adding *blocking*, see page 21, between the ends of the cut joist or an endcap to stiffen the cut-out area is recommended to make it stronger.

In most instances, the 2-foot allowance is sufficient for these plans to be adjusted to fit most homes. But if an obstruction cuts into the deck *more than 2 feet*, other measures might have to be taken to modify construction. Keep in mind, too, that in addition to *cutting into* the deck two feet or more, you may also be required to *fill in* a recess. See page 79 for information on how to do this.

THE IMPORTANCE OF A FRAMING PLAN

A *site plan*, explained on page 17, shows the big picture: how your deck is positioned in relation to your property. Property lines, utility lines, the contour of the land and existing landscaping are the kinds of items shown on a site plan. Often, you can obtain a site plan of your property from the builder of your home or the city building department. If this is not available, carefully measure and plot distances to scale on graph paper. Use 18x24-inch size paper with ¼-inch grid. Tracing paper this size and format will come in handy when adjustments are made to plans.

A *framing plan* zeros in on the deck itself, particularly the substructure—the frame. A framing plan is the guide to building the deck safely. It designates the number of footings and where they are located; the size and location of beams and joists; size and location of posts for railings (if applicable); stair construction specifics; and how the deck is positioned according to indoor rooms, including access to the deck. In addition, a framing plan specifies the deck surface lumber, including the pattern and direction the boards will be placed. For an example of these, see the illustration on page 77.

A framing plan is drawn as an overhead view—as if you were looking straight down at the deck from

above, called a *plan view*. The substructure is always drawn from the side—called an *elevation view*, sometimes from both right and left sides of the deck.

A site plan scaled down to suit the area of the property you are working with can be used to test how a deck plan will work on your lot. Place a sheet of the 18x24 graph tracing paper over your site plan. Now draw in the deck's outline as a plan view. You will probably have to make a few adjustments to make the plan work for your site.

If you are happy with a design, if it works on your lot, and if it provides the correct entry points to your home, you can now create a framing plan for its substructure. Begin by laying a sheet of graph paper over the site plan. Draw the outline of your deck and references to your home. Fill in the structural components of the deck, including joists, beams, posts, footings, and other members or details. Use the basic charts on the opposite page to determine proper spacing between support members and to designate the correct lumber for the deck's size and shape.

By this simple procedure of carefully planning and drawing in the structural support system—and checking proper size, spacing, and load-bearing data—you can create a professional-looking framing plan. However, as a cautionary measure, we also suggest that you consult an architect, builder, and local zoning officials to make sure your plan will yield a safe, secure deck.

MODIFYING THE DECK TO FIT AN OBSTRUCTION

If an architectural element of the home interferes with your deck plan, the first step is to see exactly which supports and structural members of the deck are affected. Next, determine if any will have to be removed or relocated. Start by examining the deck's framing plan. Note the location of the posts, beams, joists and other supports. Lay tracing paper over the plan and draw in where the house and all of its architectural elements will be positioned in reference to the deck.

Adding a ledger—Wherever a section of the house cuts into the deck, you have two options to adjust the layout. One option is to add a *ledger* (see opposite page) to the house in this area. To add a ledger, use joist hangers and hang the joist from the ledger. The ledger acts as a beam replacement when it is securely fastened to the home, as shown in the illustration.

Adding additional supports—The second method permits retaining the 2-foot allowance by including additional support posts and beams. The posts and beams should be the same sizes and should follow the same support patterns as those affected by the house. Caution: Do not place posts farther apart than what is recommended. (See charts at right. Or refer to specifications in the framing plan if you purchase the blueprint package.) It is always better to have too much support than not enough.

FILLING AN OFFSET OR RECESS

One of the most common modifications made to a deck is expanding the deck area at the point where it meets the house to fill an offset or recess. This is just the opposite of modifying the deck to surround an obstruction. Instead of cutting into support posts and beams, you must *insert* additional support members.

To adjust to an offset or recess, follow the same preliminaries as with an obstruction. Begin with your deck-framing plan, whether it is one you created as discussed on page 78, or one purchased. Overlay the plan with tracing paper, then draw in where the house will be located relative to the deck. This

Species Group	Post Size (inches)	Load Area: Beam Spacing x Post Spacing (square feet)									
		36	48	60	72	84	96	108	120	132	144
1	4x4	Up to 12' →→→→→→					Up to 10'		Up to 8'		
	4x6				Up to 12' →→→→				Up to 10'		
	6x6									Up to 12'	
2	4x4	Up to 12'	Up to 10' →→→→				Up to 8' →→→				
	4x6			Up to 12' →→→→			Up to 10' →→				
	6x6							Up to 12' →→			
3	4x4	Up to 12'									
			Up to 10' →→	Up to 8' →→→		Up to 6' →→→→→→→					
	4x6		Up to 12' →→	Up to 10' →→		Up to 8' →→→→→					
	6x6			Up to 12' →→→→→→→→→→							

MAXIMUM POST SIZES (Wood Beam Supports)
Based on 40 psf deck live load plus 10 psf dead load. Grade is Standard and better for 4x4 inch posts and No. 1 and better for larger sizes. Group 1—Douglas fir, larch and southern pine; Group 2—hem fir and Douglas fir south; Group 3—western pines and cedars, redwood and spruces. Example: If the beam supports are spaced 8 feet 6 inches on center, and the posts are 11 feet 6 inches, then the load area is 98. Use next larger area: 108.

Species Group	Joist Size (inches)	Joist Spacing (inches)		
		16	24	32
1	2x6	9' 9''	7' 11''	6' 2''
	2x8	12' 10''	10' 6''	8' 1''
	2x10	16' 5''	13' 4''	10' 4''
2	2x6	8' 7''	7' 0''	5' 8''
	2x8	11' 4''	9' 3''	7' 6''
	2x10	14' 6''	11' 10''	9' 6''
3	2x6	7' 9''	6' 2''	5' 0''
	2x8	10' 2''	8' 1''	6' 8''
	2x10	13' 0''	10' 4''	8' 6''

JOIST SPACING (Decking Spans)
Joists are on edge. Spans are center-to-center distances between beams or supports. Based on 40 psf deck live loads plus 10 psf dead load. Grade is No. 2 or better; No. 2 medium-grain southern pine. Group 1—Douglas fir, larch, and southern pine; Group 2—hem fir and Douglas fir south; Group 3—western pines and cedars, redwood and spruces.

Species Group	Maximum Allowable Span (inches)					
	Laid Flat				Laid on Edge	
	1x6	2x3	2x4	2x6	2x3	2x4
1	24	28	32	48	84	96
2	16	24	28	42	72	84
3	16	24	24	36	60	72

MAXIMUM ALLOWABLE SPANS FOR SPACED DECK BOARDS
These spans are based on the assumption that more than one floor board carries normal loads. If concentrated loads are a rule, spans should be reduced accordingly. Group 1—Douglas fir, larch and southern pine; Group 2—hem fir and Douglas fir south; Group 3—western pines and cedars, redwood and spruces. Based on construction grade or better (Select Structural Appearance, No. 1 or No. 2).

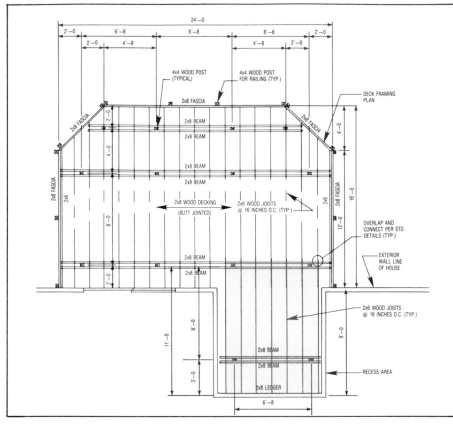

FILLING AN OFFSET OR RECESS
(See explanation for detailed information.)

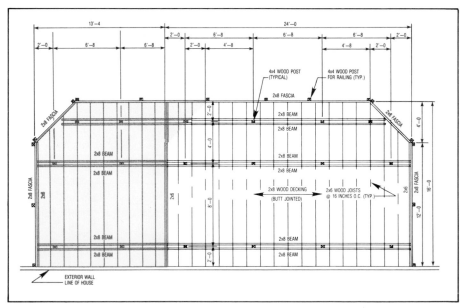

EXPANDING THE DECK LATERALLY
(See explanation for detailed information)

creates a clear picture of how much recess or offset must be filled.

Now closely examine the framing plan. You'll notice the first posts and beam are to be located two feet from the house. The size of the recess will determine how to handle the problem further.

If recess or offset is four feet or less—The best way to handle this situaton is to add a ledger. Use longer deck joists and hang them from the ledger. If the joist cannot be purchased for the length required, splice over the first support beam from the house.

If recess or offset is more than four feet—In this case, it is recommended that you add posts and a beam in the same pattern and spans as shown on the deck framing plan. Again, never increase the span of the joist between beams for lengths longer than those shown on the deck framing plan.

Step-by-step example—If the recess is 9 feet, then measure 11 feet, which includes the distance allowed from the first support posts and beam. For this example, we'll assume the widest span on the deck framing plan is 8 feet. Beginning at the existing posts and beam (located 2 feet from your home), continue placing the posts and beams at 8-foot intervals into the recess. There is now 3 feet of support structure remaining. To accommodate this, you could add a ledger to support the joist for the remaining 3 feet. Or you could place the deck 1 foot from the house and install an end header. Never extend the joist over the underlying support beam more than 2 feet without additional support. See illustration at left.

EXPANDING THE DECK LATERALLY

Your situation may require the deck to be expanded from side to side. In some instances this would not be feasible due to the physical layout of the deck. Sometimes it may not be a good idea from an aesthetic or design point of view—the deck just might not look right. Often, however, a deck can be extended at the ends or enlarged in the middle without affecting its appearance.

Step-by-step example—Remember the basic guidelines as discussed on pages 77–80, and expanding a deck laterally will be not be a problem. Refer to the deck framing plan. Use the same post sizes and the same spacing between posts. Use the same beam sizes and the same spacing between beams. Use the same joist sizes and the same spacing between joists. If you follow the deck framing plan as a maximum spacing guide for members and a minimum lumber size, you should be able to expand a deck in any direction without jeopardizing structural stability.

To expand the deck on the sides, first overlay the existing framing plan with a piece of tracing paper, as mentioned previously. Review size and location of existing framing posts and beams. Suppose, for example, you want to extend one end of the deck an additional 14 feet, and the existing posts are on 6'8" centers. Match the existing post pattern with new posts—also 6'8" away. You now have 2'8" of deck remaining to support. Because you never overhang framing more than 2 feet, you have two ways to provide the necessary support. One, make the total lateral addition 13'4" and then add two sets of posts. Or two, add a third set of posts at the end of the 2'8" span. Either method will give the deck the support it requires. See illustration on opposite page.

ADAPTING A DECK TO A SLOPE

If the proposed site for your deck slopes up or down, you will need to adjust the individual height of each of the deck's support posts as the situation requires. One method is to extend the height of posts to reach above the deck level. Next, use a line with a plumb level or a chalk line—parallel to the deck level—to determine the correct height of each post. Subtract the thickness of the beam that is to go on top of the post, and cut off the post at this level. Note: Posts can sometimes be used as railing supports if extended above the level of the deck. Plan for this accordingly. See page 23.

CHANGING LOCATION OF STAIRS AND TRAFFIC PATTERNS

If you are working with a set of Home Planners' blueprints, and you want to change the location of a stairway and access to the deck, lay a 18x24-inch sheet of tracing paper over the plans and draw the stairway in its new position, transposing the specifications. Make any necessary changes in railing, benches, or other deck details to accept the stairs in their new location. Also be sure the substructure remains true to what has been specified. Most important, be sure the steps remain a constant height. Riser and tread ratios, provided on page 23, must be constant and meet local codes.

Follow the same tracing and transposing procedure if you need to modify the deck to suit your home's indoors-to-outdoors access. Double-check the framing plan to be sure the substructure remains true to what is specified. If working off your own plan, check against the specification charts on page 79.

ADDING AN ADDITIONAL LEVEL TO SINGLE-LEVEL DECK

It is simple to add a level to a single-level deck if the *second level* is to be elevated above the original. Install footings and joists for the new deck area as if the deck was to be extended. To elevate the deck section, add an additional set of joists on top of the first set, and align them cross-wise. Nail down decking surface boards as usual. Doubling the joists will increase the height of the deck to about the right height for a step—about 7 inches.

Adding a smaller deck section that is lower or reached by steps is a little more involved. Several pre-planned multi-level decks are shown in Chapter 3. Essentially, the lower deck is designed separately from the original level, but footings can be located as if the deck were one level. To accomplish the change in elevation, adjust the size of the support posts accordingly. If the drop in elevation to the second, lower deck is designed to be a step, for safety's sake, maintain the drop at 6 to 9 inches.

CREATING A CANTILEVERED DECK

This construction technique is often used on hillside decks. It can also be used with low-level designs so the deck's substructure is placed out of sight. A cantilevered deck appears to float above the ground, since the support structure is set back away from the edge of the deck. To create this effect, the designated spans of joists and beams can be cantilevered *one-half* of the distance indicated on your framing plan. For example, if the span for joists is eight feet, they can be cantilevered four feet from the end beam. Check local codes to be certain this is allowable in your area.

OUTDOOR AMENITIES: WAYS TO CUSTOMIZE YOUR DECK

Part of the fun of building a deck is "furnishing" it, much like a room. Because a deck is an outdoor room, the add-ons and amenities

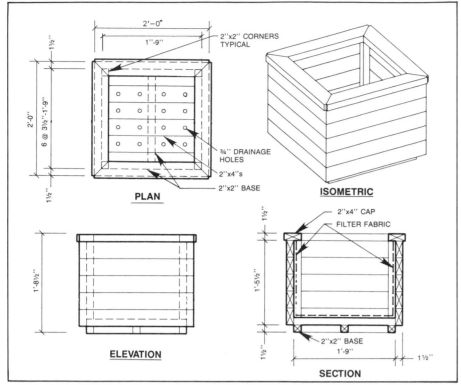

PLANTER DETAILS

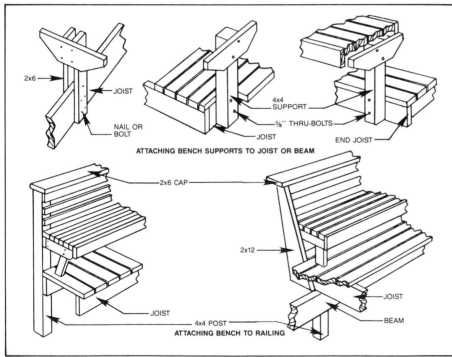

BENCH DETAILS

are different than those indoors, but the principle remains the same: to increase the comfort and livability of your deck.

One of the most exciting means of customizing your deck is to add lighting. Lighting not only allows more use of the deck during evening hours, it increases its safety. In fact, lighting stairways and steps is highly recommended to prevent potential mishaps. Lighting creates drama and evokes a festive atmosphere. Trees and shrubs become sculptural focal points with spotlight treatment. Placing lights so they shine up into the branches or foliage, *uplighting,* often produces the best effect. Don't forget, too, to add an electrical outlet or two that can be accessed on the deck. Outlets will come in handy for a number of uses such as electronic gear and power tools.

Adding a water fixture is another practical way to enhance deck-side living. A single hose bib should be sufficient, or you can add plumbing and a food preparation sink, if desired.

Note that separate building permits are required for both electricity and plumbing. Plan on getting these early on if water and power are on your want list.

GAZEBOS, STORAGE, AND OVERHEADS

These kinds of small structures on or near the deck simply make the deck more versatile. A gazebo serves as a interesting focal point, as well as a sheltered retreat. An overhead covering will certainly be appreciated during the summer months, no matter where you live. In some sections of the country, such as in the warm Southwest, shade becomes mandatory. Inexpensive latticework, commonly available at home centers and lumber supply outlets, supported by a sturdy, overhead frame, creates effective shade. Training plants such as grape vines on the supports provides cool, green relief from the hot sun. Latticework is also an excellent material to create instant privacy screens, or to designate use areas. Instead of building a frame overhead, simply create a vertical frame to serve as support for the latticework sections (usually 2x8 or 4x8.) Storage areas located under benches or under the deck itself are ideal spots to keep firewood, extra chairs, cushions or recreation gear, allowing for easy access yet out-of-sight storage.

PLANTERS, BENCHES, BARBECUES AND MORE

Many of the deck plans in this book include built-in benches.

These provide adequate outdoor seating and serve to designate various use areas on the deck. Benches are, of course, handy for relaxation. If you are going to use your deck for parties and entertaining, plan ahead and include enough benches to provide seating for average-size gatherings.

Adding plants to a deck helps soften the edges, and serves as a transition from deck to outdoor landscaping. Built-in planter boxes near the deck's perimeter also act as points of definition and help "close off" the outdoor room. Add a drip system, concealing the tubing beneath the decking. The result will be an attractive, almost automatic container garden.

Adding built-in barbecues, firepits, outdoor bars and sinks are just a few additional ideas for upgrading your deck. Many of these can be added at your leisure; others require thought ahead of time—while the deck is still in the planning stages. Electricity and plumbing, as mentioned, should be installed early on. Visualize how you are going to spend your time deck-side, and plan accordingly. For information on step-by-step plans that are available for many of these deck amenities, refer to pages 97 to 101.

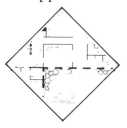

FLOOR PLANS FOR HOMES IN THIS BOOK

Though they are adaptable to any size or style of house, the deck designs in this book were created to complement homes in the Home Planners' portfolio. Pages 25 through 75 provide you with a great perspective of the deck plans featured on those pages, but only a rear view of the corresponding home plans. On the following pages are more complete illustrations of the homes, plus floor plans for your inspection. For each of the homes in this section, we offer a complete set of construction drawings and a materials list so you can build your own home or work with a contractor or architect to have it built. For more information about these blueprint packages or other fine products available from Home Planners, Inc., please turn to page 106 or call toll-free 800-521-6797.

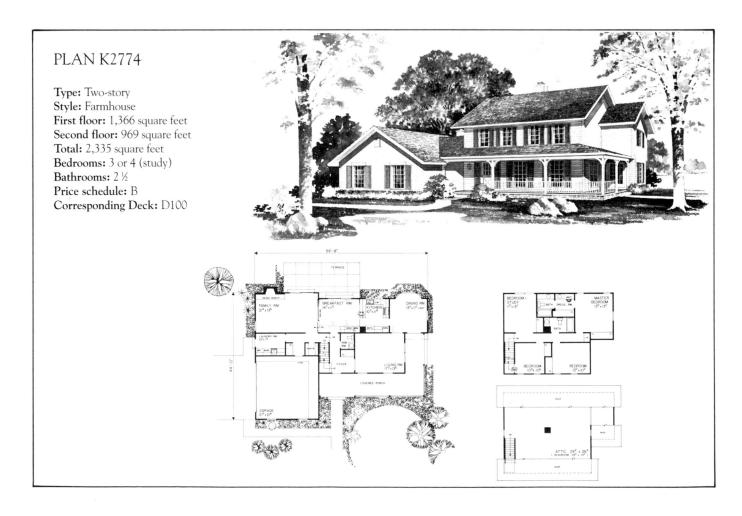

PLAN K2774

Type: Two-story
Style: Farmhouse
First floor: 1,366 square feet
Second floor: 969 square feet
Total: 2,335 square feet
Bedrooms: 3 or 4 (study)
Bathrooms: 2 ½
Price schedule: B
Corresponding Deck: D100

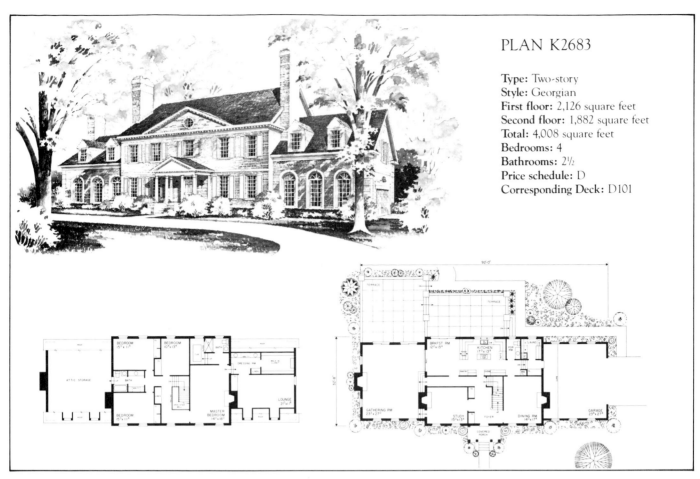

PLAN K2683

Type: Two-story
Style: Georgian
First floor: 2,126 square feet
Second floor: 1,882 square feet
Total: 4,008 square feet
Bedrooms: 4
Bathrooms: 2½
Price schedule: D
Corresponding Deck: D101

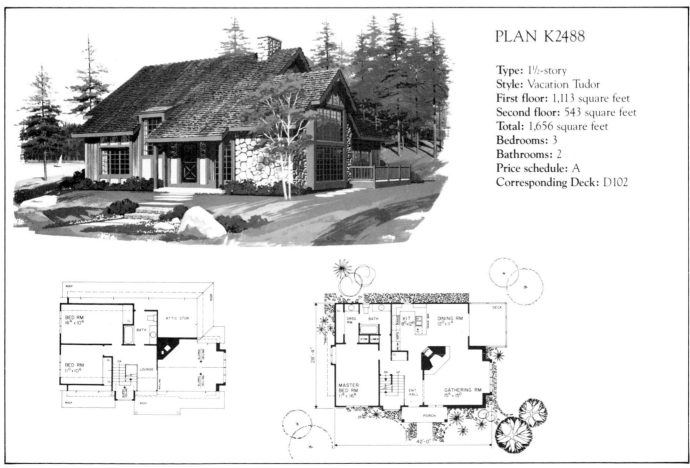

PLAN K2488

Type: 1½-story
Style: Vacation Tudor
First floor: 1,113 square feet
Second floor: 543 square feet
Total: 1,656 square feet
Bedrooms: 3
Bathrooms: 2
Price schedule: A
Corresponding Deck: D102

PLAN K2855

Type: Two-story
Style: Tudor
First floor: 1,372 square feet
Second floor: 1,245 square feet
Total: 2,617 square feet
Bedrooms: 4
Bathrooms: 2½ + powder room
Price schedule: B
Corresponding Deck: D103

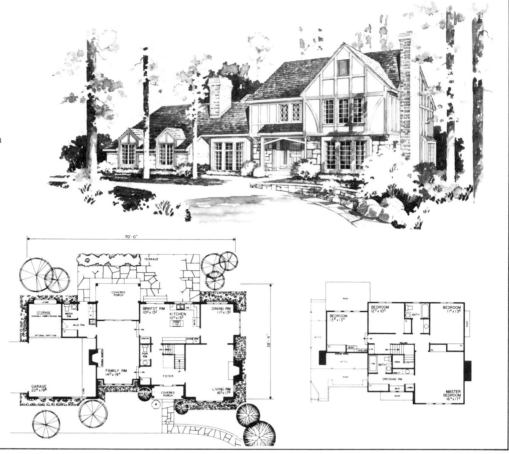

PLAN K2921

Type: 1 ½-story
Style: Cape Cod Ranch
First floor: 3,215 square feet
Second floor: 711 square feet
Total: 3,926 square feet
Bedrooms: 3
Bathrooms: 2 ½+ washroom
Price schedule: D
Corresponding Deck: D104

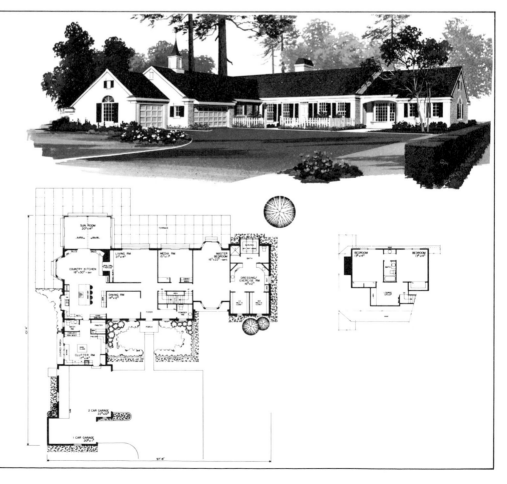

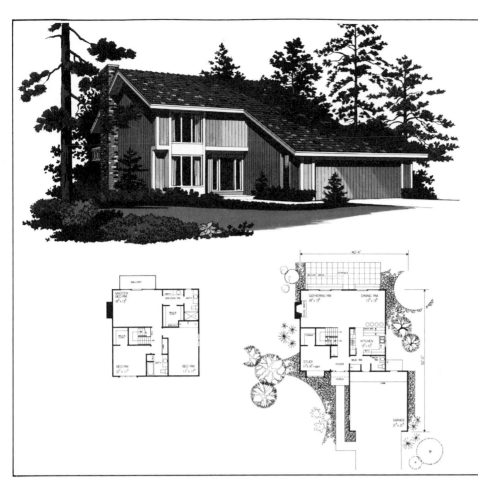

PLAN K2711

Type: Two-story
Style: Contemporary
First floor: 975 square feet
Second floor: 1,024 square feet
Total: 1,999 square feet
Bedrooms: 3
Bathrooms: 2½
Price schedule: B
Corresponding Deck: D105

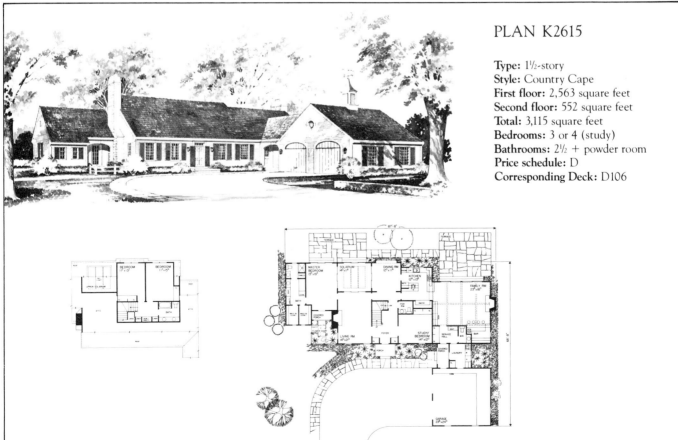

PLAN K2615

Type: 1½-story
Style: Country Cape
First floor: 2,563 square feet
Second floor: 552 square feet
Total: 3,115 square feet
Bedrooms: 3 or 4 (study)
Bathrooms: 2½ + powder room
Price schedule: D
Corresponding Deck: D106

PLAN K2543

Type: Two-story
Style: French
First floor: 2,345 square feet
Second floor: 1,687 square feet
Total: 4,032 square feet
Bedrooms: 4
Bathrooms: 3½ + powder room
Price schedule: D
Corresponding Deck: D107

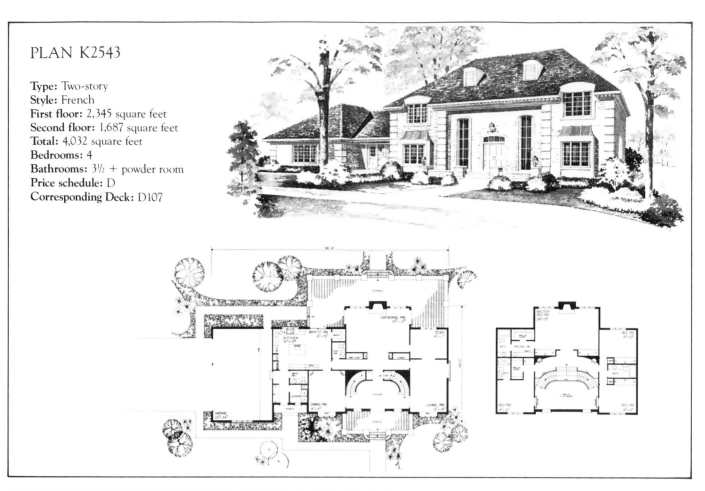

PLAN K2511

Type: Multi-level
Style: Contemporary Hillside
Main level: 1,043 square feet
Upper level: 703 square feet
Lower level: 794 square feet
Total: 2,540 square feet
Bedrooms: 3 or 4 (study)
Bathrooms: 3
Price schedule: B
Corresponding Deck: D108

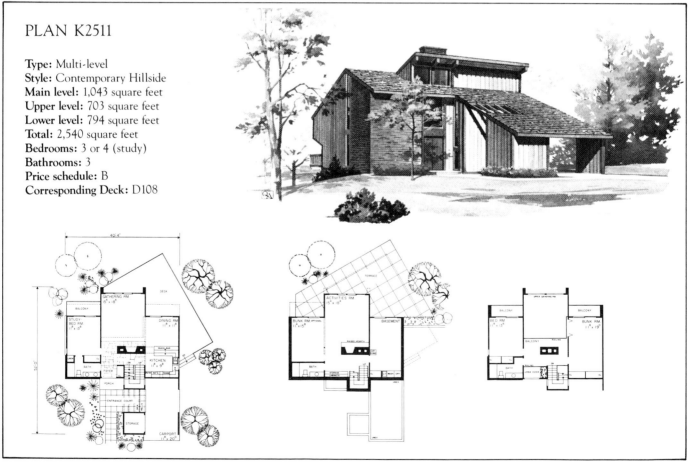

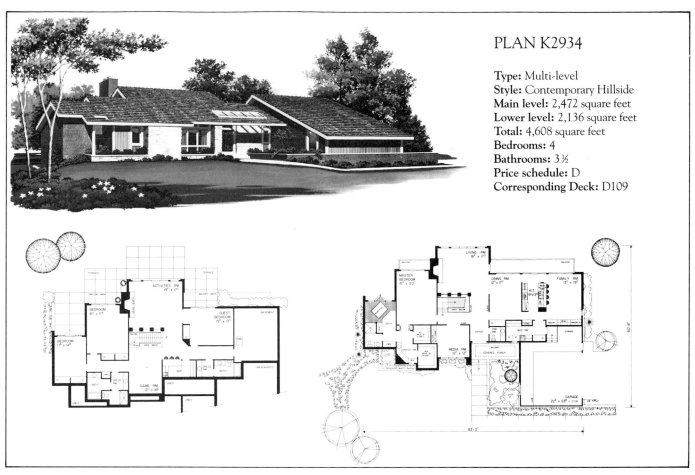

PLAN K2934

Type: Multi-level
Style: Contemporary Hillside
Main level: 2,472 square feet
Lower level: 2,136 square feet
Total: 4,608 square feet
Bedrooms: 4
Bathrooms: 3 ½
Price schedule: D
Corresponding Deck: D109

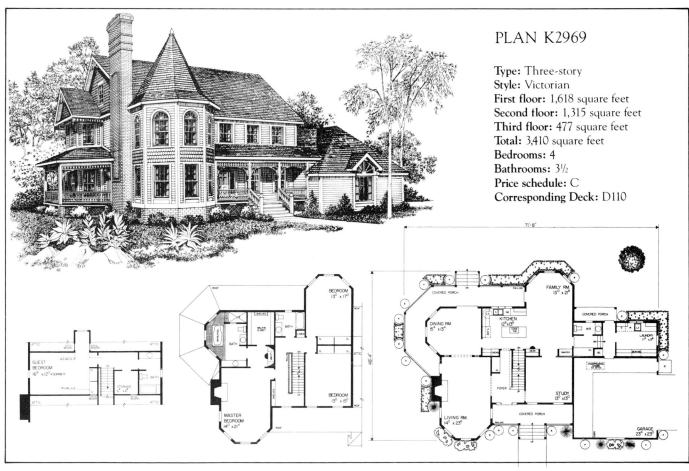

PLAN K2969

Type: Three-story
Style: Victorian
First floor: 1,618 square feet
Second floor: 1,315 square feet
Third floor: 477 square feet
Total: 3,410 square feet
Bedrooms: 4
Bathrooms: 3½
Price schedule: C
Corresponding Deck: D110

PLAN K2953

Type: Two-story
Style: Victorian
First floor: 2,995 square feet
Second floor: 1,831 square feet
Total: 4,826 square feet
Bedrooms: 5
Bathrooms: 4½ + powder room
Price schedule: E
Corresponding Deck: D111

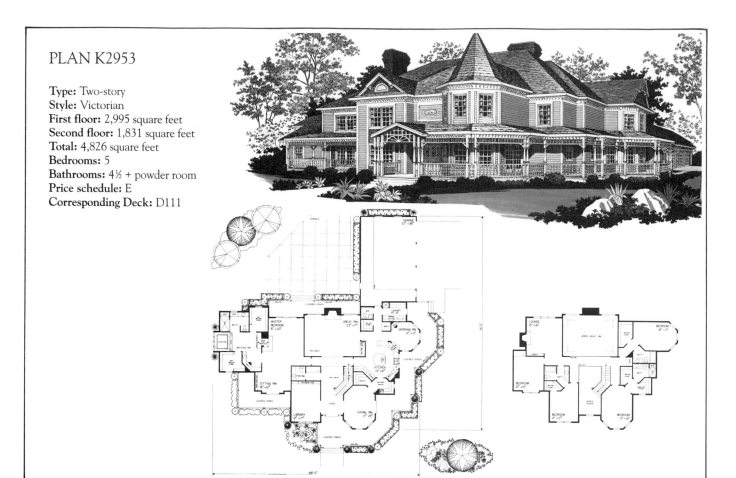

PLAN K2941/2943

Type: One-story
Style: Optional Elevations
Square footage: 1,834
Bedrooms: 2
Bathrooms: 2
Price schedule: B
Also available with a Tudor
exterior—K2942.
Corresponding Deck: D112

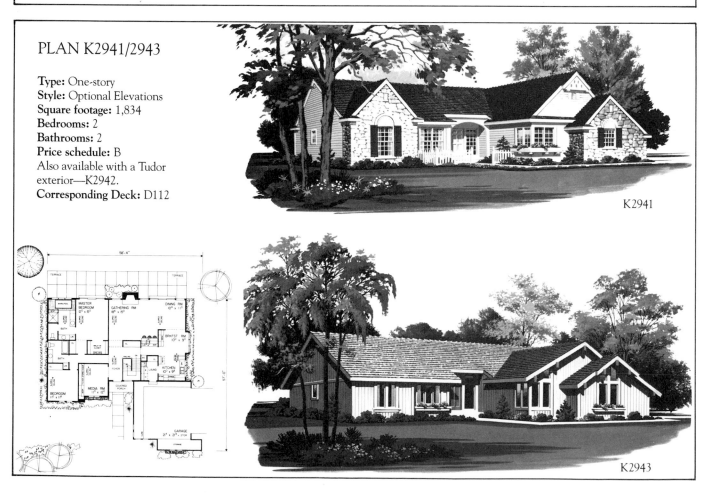

K2941

K2943

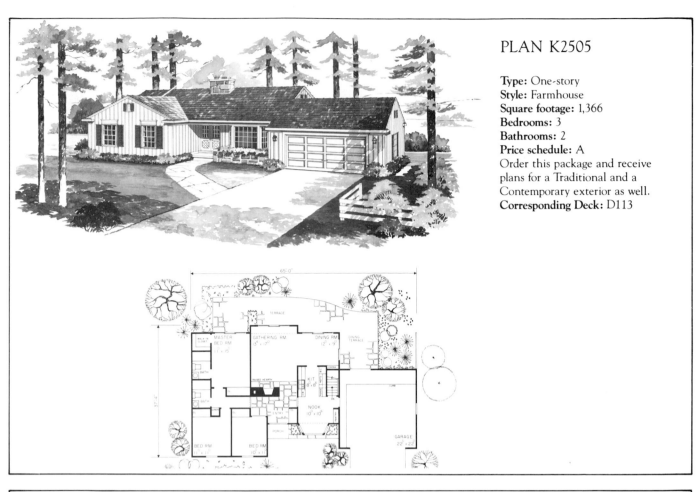

PLAN K2505

Type: One-story
Style: Farmhouse
Square footage: 1,366
Bedrooms: 3
Bathrooms: 2
Price schedule: A
Order this package and receive plans for a Traditional and a Contemporary exterior as well.
Corresponding Deck: D113

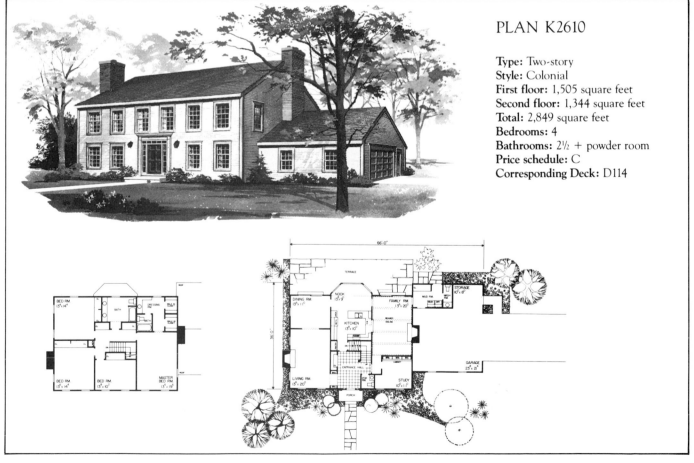

PLAN K2610

Type: Two-story
Style: Colonial
First floor: 1,505 square feet
Second floor: 1,344 square feet
Total: 2,849 square feet
Bedrooms: 4
Bathrooms: 2½ + powder room
Price schedule: C
Corresponding Deck: D114

PLAN K2682

Type: 1½-story
Style: Expandable Cape Cod
First floor: 976 square feet (basic plan); 1,230 square feet (expanded plan)
Second floor: 744 (both plans)
Total: 1,720 square feet (basic plan); 1,974 square feet (expanded plan)
Bedrooms: 3
Bathrooms: 2½
Price schedule: A
Corresponding Deck: D115

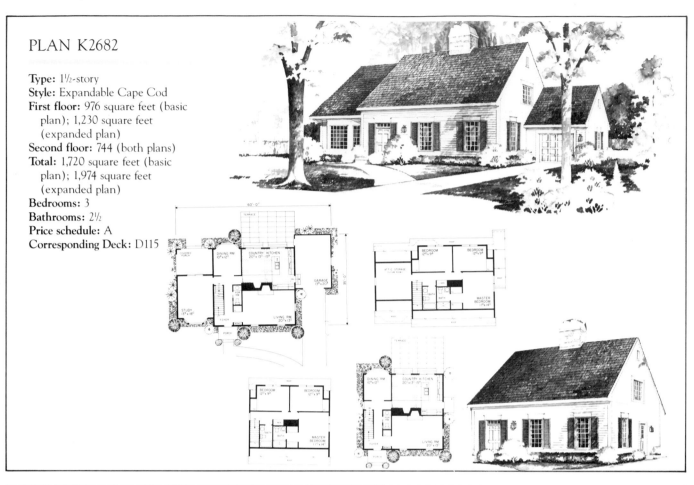

PLAN K2826

Type: Two-story
Style: Neo-Traditional
First floor: 1,112 square feet
Second floor: 881 square feet
Total: 1,993 square feet
Bedrooms: 3
Bathrooms: 2½
Price schedule: B
Corresponding Deck: D116

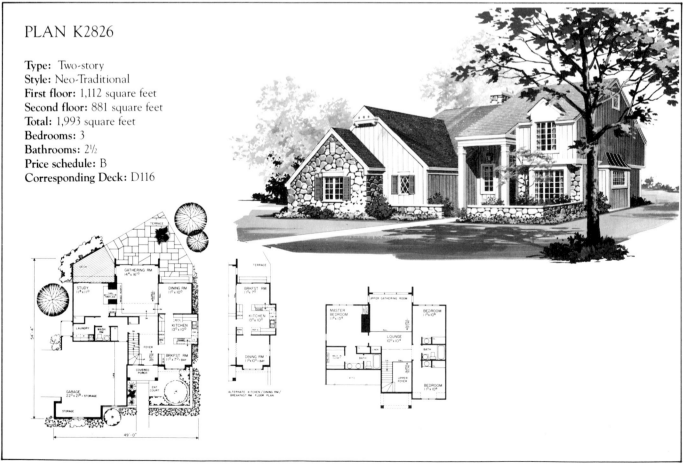

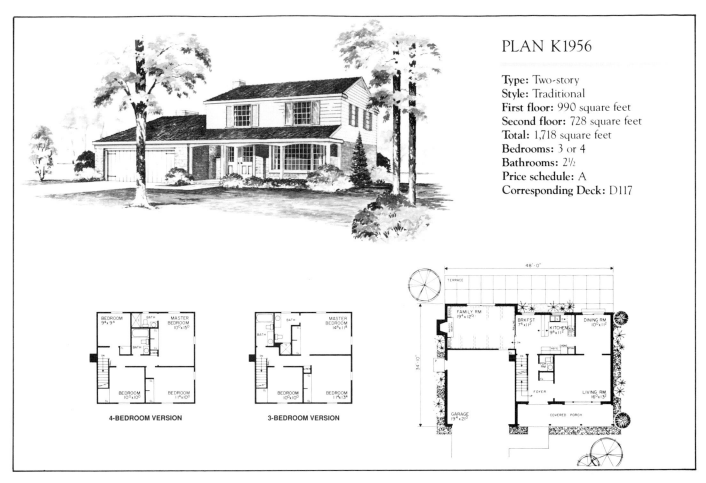

PLAN K1956

Type: Two-story
Style: Traditional
First floor: 990 square feet
Second floor: 728 square feet
Total: 1,718 square feet
Bedrooms: 3 or 4
Bathrooms: 2½
Price schedule: A
Corresponding Deck: D117

4-BEDROOM VERSION

3-BEDROOM VERSION

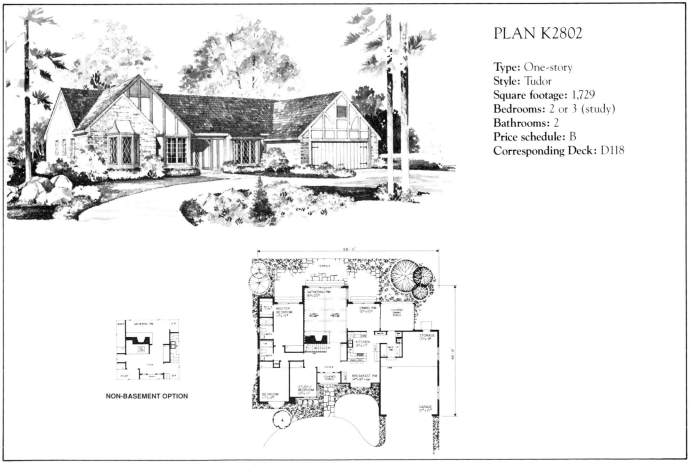

PLAN K2802

Type: One-story
Style: Tudor
Square footage: 1,729
Bedrooms: 2 or 3 (study)
Bathrooms: 2
Price schedule: B
Corresponding Deck: D118

NON-BASEMENT OPTION

PLAN K2356

Type: Two-story
Style: Tudor
First floor: 1,969 square feet
Second floor: 1,702 square feet
Total: 3,671 square feet
Bedrooms: 5
Bathrooms: 3½
Price schedule: D
Corresponding Deck: D119

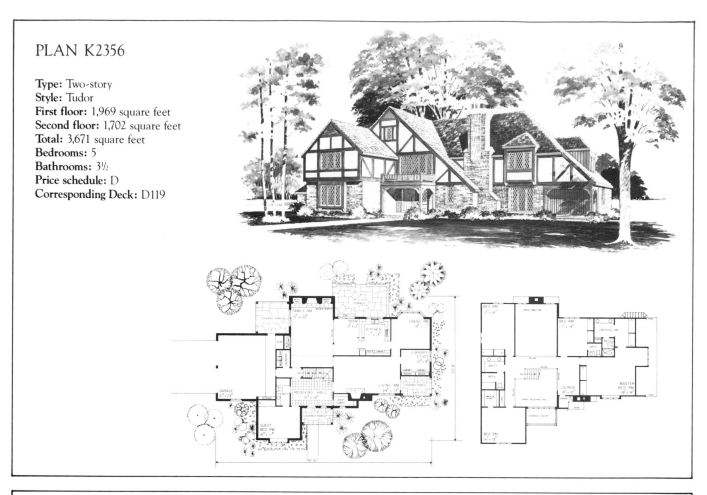

PLAN K2379

Type: Two-story
Style: Western Contemporary
First floor: 1,525 square feet
Second floor: 748 square feet
Total: 2,273 square feet
Bedrooms: 3 or 4 (study)
Bathrooms: 3
Price schedule: B
Corresponding Deck: D120

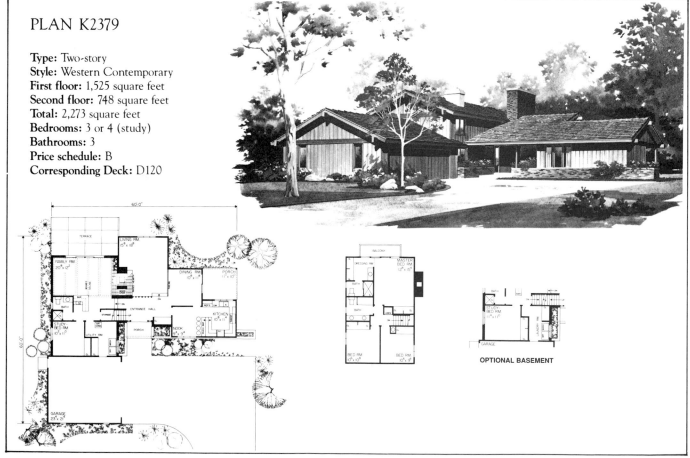

OPTIONAL BASEMENT

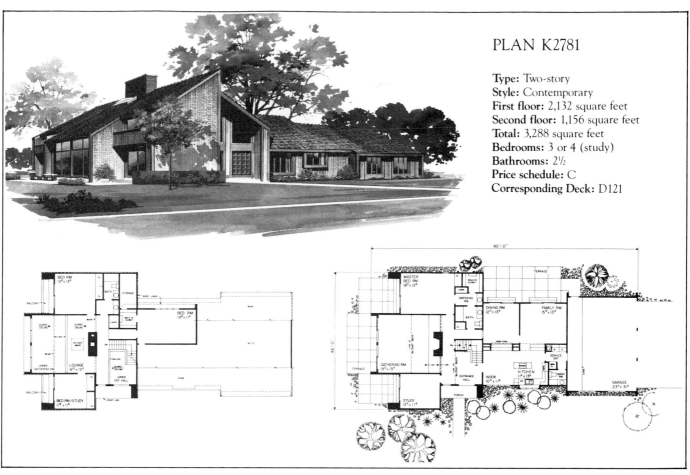

PLAN K2781

Type: Two-story
Style: Contemporary
First floor: 2,132 square feet
Second floor: 1,156 square feet
Total: 3,288 square feet
Bedrooms: 3 or 4 (study)
Bathrooms: 2½
Price schedule: C
Corresponding Deck: D121

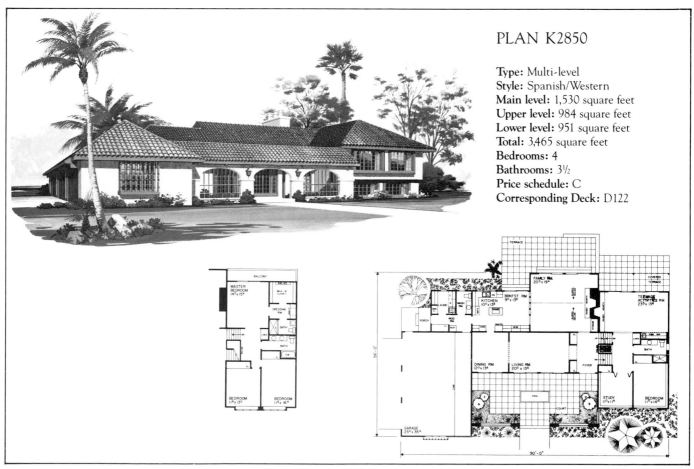

PLAN K2850

Type: Multi-level
Style: Spanish/Western
Main level: 1,530 square feet
Upper level: 984 square feet
Lower level: 951 square feet
Total: 3,465 square feet
Bedrooms: 4
Bathrooms: 3½
Price schedule: C
Corresponding Deck: D122

PLAN K2949

Type: One-story
Style: Southwestern
Square footage: 2,922
Bedrooms: 2
Bathrooms: 2½
Price schedule: C
Corresponding Deck: D123

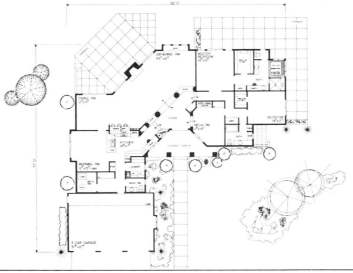

PLAN K2913

Type: One-story
Style: Contemporary
Square footage: 1,835
Bedrooms: 2
Bathrooms: 2
Price schedule: B
Corresponding Deck: D124

OUTDOOR AMENITIES

No house should go empty-landed for long. If you're searching for just the right structure to fill up those wide open spaces, we've got some great choices to show you: Among others, you'll find a get-away-from-it-all gazebo that's big enough for small gatherings, an ultra-relaxing whirlpool and sauna combination, a delightful stable that is flexible enough to serve a variety of other purposes, and a gorgeous little crafts cottage with one very bright touch. For information on how to order these plans, turn to page 111 or call us toll-free 800-521-6797.

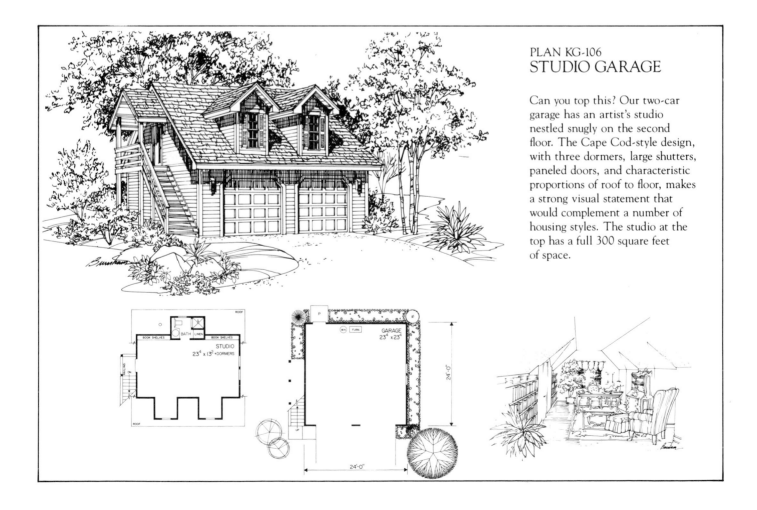

PLAN KG-106
STUDIO GARAGE

Can you top this? Our two-car garage has an artist's studio nestled snugly on the second floor. The Cape Cod-style design, with three dormers, large shutters, paneled doors, and characteristic proportions of roof to floor, makes a strong visual statement that would complement a number of housing styles. The studio at the top has a full 300 square feet of space.

PLAN KG-108
NEO-CLASSIC GAZEBO

Our gazebo is a prime spot for entertaining. At 200-plus square feet of decking, it has as much surface space as the average family room. Plus it's just under 17½ feet tall, which makes it the size of a typical one-story house. It features perfect proportions, columns, and bases that match it well with many home styles.

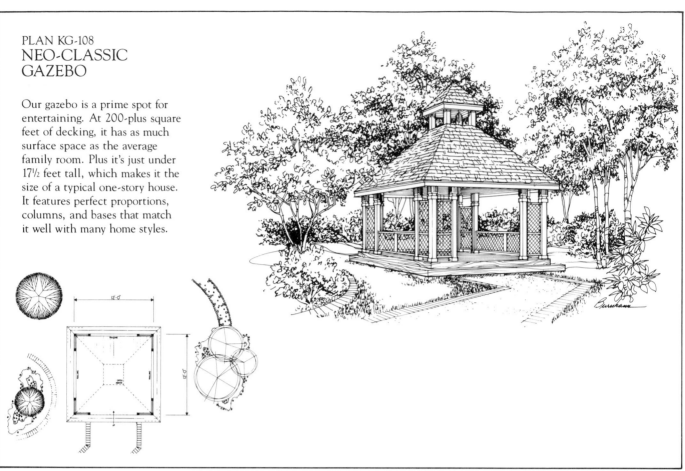

PLAN KG-109
CRAFT COTTAGE

Great space for a cottage industry, this little building (250 square feet) is both functional and good looking. Ample counter space and shelving provide plenty of room to work. Next to the work space is a cozy sun room. French doors and plenty of windows (including a circle-head version) bathe the room in light while overhangs offer adequate shading.

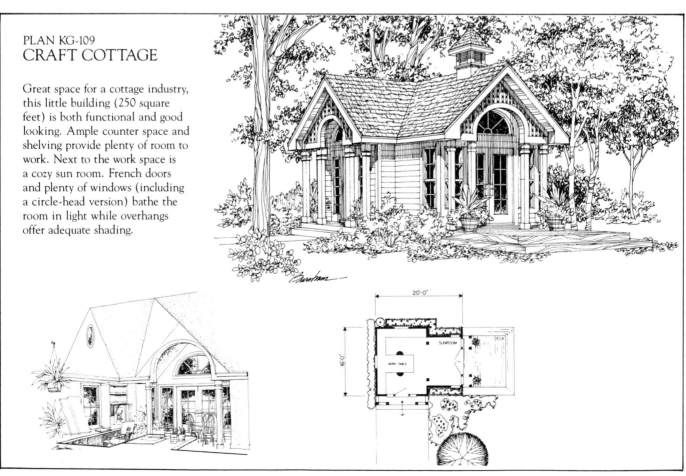

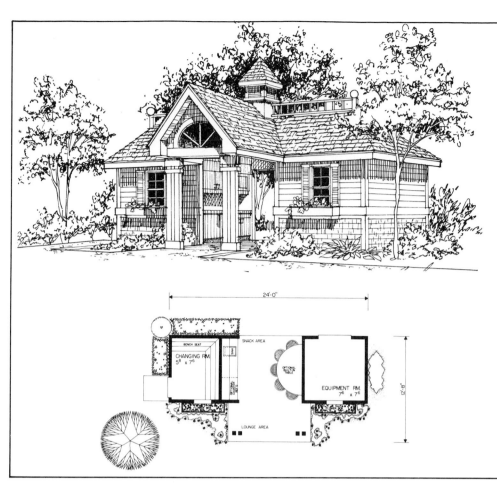

PLAN KG-110
POOL CABANA

Imagine this charming structure perched adjacent to your back-yard swimming pool. Its high-lights feature hip and gable roofs, a decorative cupola, shuttered windows, flower boxes, and horizontal wood and shingle siding. A spacious sheltered party/lounge area has a counter, sink, and refrigerator space. The equal-sized rooms provide a convenient changing area and handy equipment storage.

PLAN KG-113
COUNTRY STABLE

Charming, cross-braced Dutch doors and a steepled roof are fitting details for this free-standing stable. There's room for two horses and all their tack. The covered porch on the stall side acts as a weather buffer, keeping rain and hot sun away from precious animals. Shuttered windows are accented with window boxes. Simple modifications turn the structure into a writer's cottage or gardening workshop.

PLAN KG-111
WORKSHOP GARAGE

Tudor appeal is beautifully applied to a free-standing workshop garage. Distinctive roof lines, simulated beam work, stucco, and stone set the character. Three garage doors allow for flexible access to the two areas; a skylight provides an extra measure of natural light. Storage for lumber above the workshop is found in an out-of-the-way loft. Additional storage is reached via disappearing stairs in the garage.

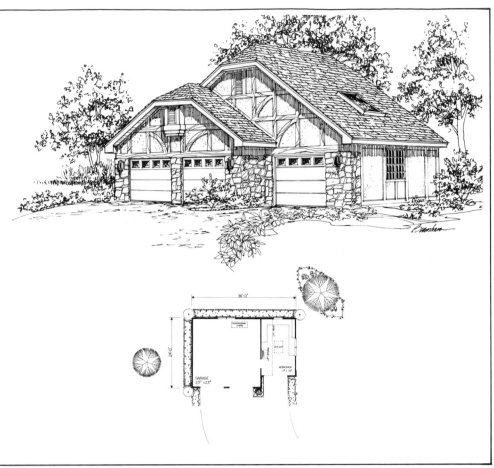

PLAN KG-112
SOOTHING WHIRL-POOL/SAUNA

A relaxing addition to back-yard space, this sauna and whirlpool spa combination promises respite from the hectic world. Joined to the house by wooden decking and a sun-filtering trellis, the dry heat sauna has planked seating as well as a sink and shower, and bench seating in the dressing area. Just outside, raised planters flank the spa on two sides. The third side has a long bench seat.

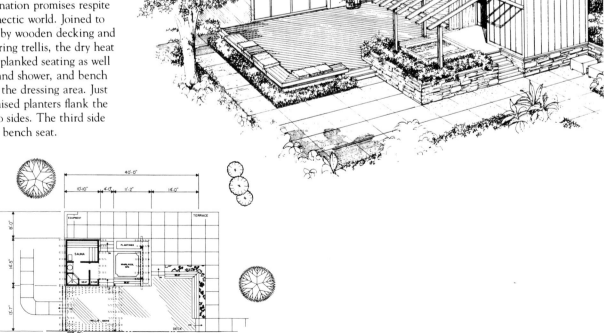

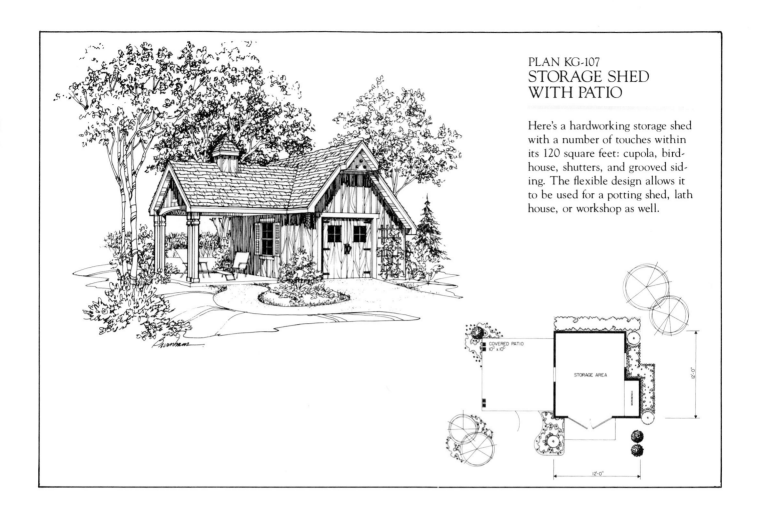

PLAN KG-107
STORAGE SHED
WITH PATIO

Here's a hardworking storage shed with a number of touches within its 120 square feet: cupola, birdhouse, shutters, and grooved siding. The flexible design allows it to be used for a potting shed, lath house, or workshop as well.

COVERED PATIO
10⁰ x 10⁰

STORAGE AREA

WORKBENCH

12'-0"

12'-0"

The Deck Blueprint Package

Our plans and details are carefully prepared in an easy-to-understand format that will guide you through every stage of your deck-building project. The Deck Blueprint Package contains four sheets outlining information pertinent to the specific Deck Plan you have chosen. A separate package — Deck Construction Details — provides the how-to data for building any deck, including instructions for adaptations and conversions.

Standard Details for Building Your Deck

In five information-packed sheets, these standard details provide all the general data necessary for building, adapting, and converting any deck. Included are layout examples, framing patterns, and foundation variation; details for ledgers, columns, and beams; schedules and charts; handrail, stair, and ramp details; and special options like spa platforms, planters, bars, benches and overhead trellises. This is a must-have package for the first-time deck builder and a useful addition to the custom deck plans shown on the next pages. Only $14.95. Also available, our Complete Deck Building Package containing 1 set of Custom Deck Plans of your choice, plus 1 set of Standard Deck Building Details all for one low price.

Custom Deck Plans

Each deck plan shown on pages 26 to 74 has been custom-designed by a professional architect. With each Custom Deck Plan, you receive the following:

Deck Plan Frontal Sheet. An artist's line drawing shows the deck as it connects to its matching or corresponding house. This drawing provides a visual image of what the deck will look like when completed, highlighting the livability factors.

Deck Framing and Floor Plans. In clear, easy-to-read drawings, this sheet shows all component parts of the deck from an aerial viewpoint with dimensions, notes, and references. Drawn at 1/4" = 1' - 0", the floor plan provides a finished overhead view of the deck including rails, stairs, benches, and ramps. The framing plan gives complete details on how the deck is to be built, including the position and spacing of footings, joists, beams, posts, and decking materials. Where necessary, the sheet also includes sections and closeups to further explain structural details.

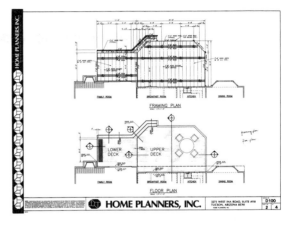

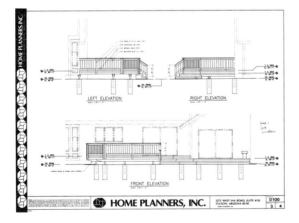

Deck Materials List. This is a complete shopping list of all the materials needed (including sizes and amounts) to build your deck. The Materials List is complemented by section drawings showing placement of hardware such as thru-bolts, screws, nuts, washers, and nails and how these items are used to secure deck flooring, rails, posts, and joists. Scale is 3/4" = 1' - 0".

Deck Elevations. Large-scale front and side elevations of the deck complete the visual picture of the deck. Drawn at 3/8" = 1' - 0", the elevations show the height of rails, balusters, stair risers, benches and other deck accessories.

QUANTITY	SIZE	DESCRIPTION
	MATERIAL LIST	
23	4"x4" - 4'	TREATED LUMBER
12	4"X4" - 5'	TREATED LUMBER
52 L.F.	2"x2"	TREATED BALUSTERS 30" LG.
300 L.F.	2"x4"	TREATED LUMBER
1850 L.F.	2"x6"	TREATED LUMBER
600 L.F.	2"x8"	TREATED LUMBER
10 L.F.	2"x10"	TREATED LUMBER
8 L.F.	2"x12"	TREATED LUMBER
70 L.F.		LANDSCAPE EDGE
550 S.F.		FILTER FABRIC
550 S.F.		2" DEEP PEA GRAVEL
60	3/8"øx8" LG.	THRU-BOLTS W/ NUTS & WASHERS
30	3/8"øx6" LG.	THRU-BOLTS W/ NUTS & WASHERS
4		1 1/2"x1 1/2"x1/8"-7" LG. STEEL ANGLES
16	3/16"øx2"	LAG SCREWS
2 LBS.	8d	FOR RAILINGS
5 LBS.	16d	FOR POSTS & JOISTS
25 LBS.	10d	FOR DECKING
		NOTE: ALL NAILS TO BE HOT DIPPED GALVANIZED SCREW NAILS
		*QUANTITY OF NAILS MAY VARY DEPENDING ON TYPE OF CONNECTIONS USED.

TO ORDER, CALL TOLL FREE 1-800-521-6797, OR SEE PAGE 105.

Deck Plan Index

Deck Plans Price Schedule

CUSTOM DECK PLANS

Price Group	Q	R	S
1 Set Custom Plans	$25	$30	$35

    Additional identical sets ....$10 each
    Reverse sets (mirror image)..$10 each

STANDARD DECK DETAILS

1 Set Generic Construction Details .... $14.95 each

COMPLETE DECK BUILDING PACKAGE

Price Group	Q	R	S
1 Set Custom Plans, plus			
1 Set Standard Deck Details	$35	$40	$45

◘ Deck Blueprint Order Form

TO ORDER: Find the Deck Plan number in the Plans Index (opposite). Consult the Price Schedule (opposite) to determine the price of your plan, adding any additional or reverse sets you desire. Or specify the Complete Building Package which contains 1 set of Custom Deck Plans of your choice, plus 1 set of Standard Deck Building Details. Complete the Order Coupon on this page and mail with your check or money order. If you prefer, you can also use a credit card. Please include the correct postage and handling fees.

Our Service Policy
We try to process and ship every order from our office within 48 hours. For this reason, we won't send a formal notice acknowledging receipt of your order.

Our Exchange Policy
Because we produce and ship plans in response to individual orders, we cannot honor requests for refunds. However, you can exchange your entire order of blueprints, including a single set if you order just one, for a set of another deck design. All exchanges carry an additional fee of $15.00 plus $10.00 postage and handling if they're sent via Regular Service; $20.00 via 2nd Day Air; $22 Next Day Air.

About Reverse Blueprints
If you want to install your deck in reverse of the plan as shown, we will include an extra set of blueprints with the Frontal Sheet, Framing and Floor Plans, and Elevations reversed for an additional fee of $10.00. Although callouts and lettering appear backward, reverses will prove useful as a visual aid if you decide to flop the plan.

How Many Blueprints Do You Need?
To study your favorite deck plan or make alterations of the plan to fit your home, one set of Deck Blueprints may be sufficient. On the other hand, if you plan to install the deck yourself using subcontractors or have a general contractor do the work for you, you will probably need more sets. Use the checklist below to estimate the number you'll need:

Blueprint Checklist
- _____**Owner**
- _____**Deck Contractor or Subcontractor**
- _____**Building Materials Supplier**
- _____**Lender or Mortgage Source, if applicable**
- _____**Community Building Department for Permits (sometimes requires 2 sets)**
- _____**Subdivision Committee, if any**
- _____**Total Number of Sets**

Blueprint Hotline
Call Toll-Free 1-800-521-6797. We'll ship your order the following business day if you call us by 4:00 p.m. Eastern Time. When you order by phone, please be prepared to give us the Order Form Key Number shown in the box at the bottom of the Order Form. By FAX: Copy the order form at right and send on our FAX line: 1-800-224-6699 or 1-602-297-9937.

Canadian Customers
Order Toll-Free 1-800-561-4169
For faster service and plans that are modified for building in Canada, customers may now call in orders directly to our Canadian supplier of plans and charge the purchase to a charge card. Or, you may complete the order form at right, adding 30% to all prices and mail in Canadian funds to:

The Plan Centre
20 Cedar Street North
Kitchener, Ontario N2H 2W8

By FAX: Copy the Order Form on the next page and send it via our Canadian FAX line: 1-519-743-1282.

BLUEPRINTS ARE NOT RETURNABLE

HOME PLANNERS, INC.
3275 WEST INA ROAD SUITE 110,
TUCSON, ARIZONA 85741

Please rush me the following Deck Blueprints:

_____ Set(s) of Custom Deck Plan_____
(See Index and Price Schedule) \$_____

_____ Additional identical blueprints
in same order @ $10.00 per set. \$_____

_____ Reverse blueprints @ $10.00 per set. \$_____

_____ Sets of Standard Deck
Details @ $14.95 per set. \$_____

_____ Sets of Complete Building Package (Best Buy!)
Includes Custom Deck Plan_____
(see Index and Price Schedule)
Plus Standard Deck Details \$_____

POSTAGE AND HANDLING	
DELIVERY—Must have street address - No P.O. Boxes	
•Ground Service (Allow 4-6 days delivery)	❑ $ 8.00
•2nd Day Air (Allow 2-3 days delivery)	❑ $12.00
•Next Day Air (Allow 1 day delivery)	❑ $22.00
POST OFFICE DELIVERY If no street address.	
•Priority Air Mail (Allow 4-6 days delivery)	❑ $10.00
OVERSEAS DELIVERY Note: All delivery times are from date Blueprint Package is shipped.	fax, phone or mail for quote

POSTAGE (From shaded box above) \$_____

SUB-TOTAL \$_____

SALES TAX (Arizona residents add 5% sales tax; Michigan residents add 6% sales tax.) \$_____

TOTAL (Sub-total and tax) \$_____

YOUR ADDRESS (please print)
Name _____

Street_____

City_____State_____Zip_____

Daytime telephone number (_____)_____

CREDIT CARD ORDERS ONLY
Fill in the boxes below

Credit card number

Exp. Date: Month/Year

Check one ❑ Visa ❑ MasterCard ❑ Discover Card

Signature _____

Order Form Key
TB19DP

ORDER TOLL FREE
1-800-521-6797 or
602-297-8200

The Home Plans Blueprint Package...

Take a look at our complete set of high quality plans.

Building a home? Planning a home? The Blueprint Package from Home Planners, Inc. contains nearly everything you need to get the job done right, whether you're working on your own or with help from an architect, designer, builder or subcontractors. Each Blueprint Package is the result of many hours of work by licensed architects or professional designers.

QUALITY
Hundreds of hours of painstaking effort have gone into the development of your blueprint set. Each home has been quality-checked by professionals to insure accuracy and buildability.

VALUE
Because we sell in volume, you can buy professional-quality blueprints at a fraction of their development cost. With Home Planners, your dream home design costs only a few hundred dollars, not the thousands of dollars that custom architects charge.

SERVICE
Once you've chosen your favorite home plan, we stand ready to serve you with knowledgeable sales people and prompt, efficient service. We ship most orders within 48 hours of receipt and stand behind every set of blueprints we sell.

SATISFACTION
We have been in business since 1946 and have shipped over 1 million blueprints to home builders just like you. Nearly 50 years of service and hundreds of thousands of satisfied customers are your guarantee that Home Planners can do the job for you.

ORDER TOLL FREE 1-800-521-6797

After you've studied our Blueprint Package and Important Extras on the following pages, simply mail the accompanying order form on page 111 or call toll free on our Blueprint Hotline: 1-800-521-6797. We're ready and eager to serve you.

Each set of blueprints is an interrelated collection of floor plans, interior and exterior elevations, dimensions, cross-sections, diagrams and notations showing precisely how your house is to be constructed.

Here's what you get:

Frontal Sheet
This artist's sketch of the exterior of the house, done in two-point perspective, gives you an idea of how the house will look when built and landscaped. Large ink-line floor plans show all levels of the house and provide a quick overview of your new home's livability, as well as a handy reference for studying furniture placement.

Foundation Plan
Drawn to 1/4-inch scale, this sheet shows the complete foundation layout, including support

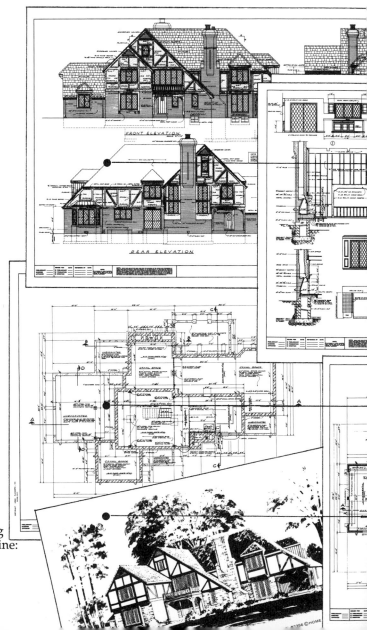

walls, excavated and unexcavated areas, if any and foundation notes. If slab construction rather than basement, the plan shows footings and details for a monolithic slab. This page, or another in the set, also includes a sample plot plan for locating your house on a building site.

Detailed Floor Plans
Complete in 1/4-inch scale, these plans show the layout of each floor of the house. All rooms and interior spaces are carefully dimensioned and keys are provided for cross-section details given later in the plans. The position of all electrical outlets and switches are clearly shown.

House Cross-Sections
Large-scale views, normally drawn at 3/8-inch equals 1 foot, show sections or cut-aways of the foundation, interior walls, exterior walls,

floors, stairways and roof details. Additional cross-sections are given to show important changes in floor, ceiling or roof heights or the relationship of one level to another. Extremely valuable for construction, these sections show exactly how the various parts of the house fit together.

Interior Elevations
These large-scale drawings show the design and placement of kitchen and bathroom cabinets, laundry areas, fireplaces, bookcases and other built-ins. Little "extras," such as mantelpiece and wainscoting drawings, plus moulding sections, provide details that give your home that custom touch.

Exterior Elevations
Drawings in 1/4-inch scale show the front, rear and sides of your house and give necessary notes on exterior materials and finishes. Particular attention is given to cornice detail, brick and stone accents or other finish items that make your home distinctive.

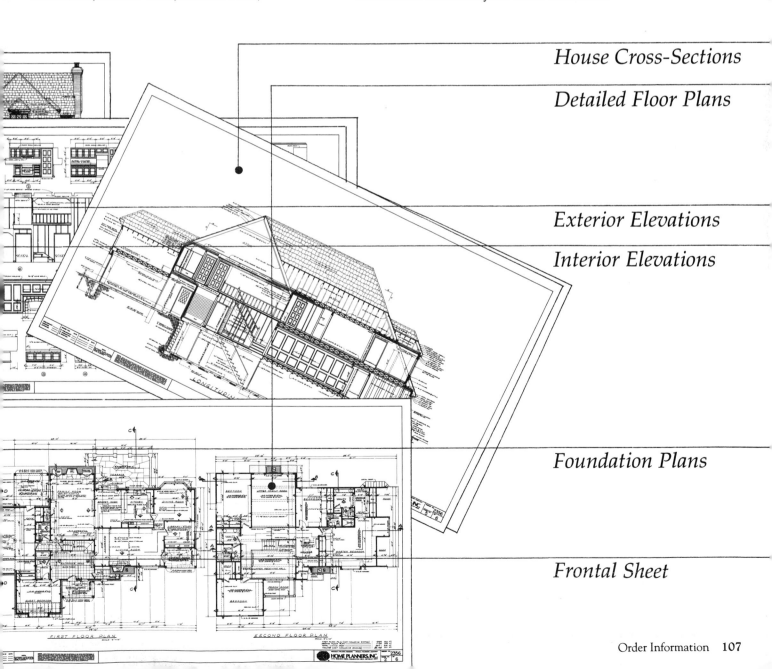

House Cross-Sections

Detailed Floor Plans

Exterior Elevations

Interior Elevations

Foundation Plans

Frontal Sheet

Important Extras To Do The Job Right!

Introducing seven important planning and construction aids developed by our professionals to help you succeed in your home-building project.

To Order, Call Toll Free 1-800-521-6797

To add these important extras to your Blueprint Package, simply indicate your choices on the order form on page 111 or call us Toll Free 1-800-521-6797 and we'll tell you more about these exciting products.

MATERIALS LIST

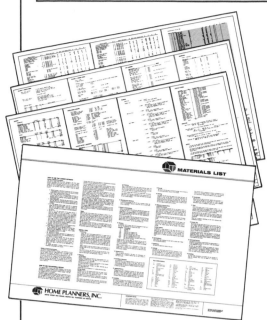

For each design in our portfolio, we offer a customized materials take-off that is invaluable in planning and estimating the cost of your new home. This comprehensive list outlines the quantity, type and size of material needed to build your house (with the exception of mechanical system items). Included are:

- framing lumber
- roofing and sheet metal
- windows and doors
- exterior sheathing material and trim
- masonry, veneer and fireplace materials
- tile and flooring materials
- kitchen and bath cabinetry
- interior drywall and trim
- rough and finish hardware
- many more items

(Note: Because of differing local codes, building methods, and availability of materials, our Materials Lists do not include mechanical materials. To obtain necessary take-offs and recommendations, consult heating, plumbing and electrical contractors. Materials Lists are not sold separately from the Blueprint Package.)

This handy list helps you or your builder cost out materials and serves as a ready reference sheet when you're compiling bids. It also provides a cross-check against the materials specified by your builder and helps coordinate the substitution of items you may need to meet local codes.

SPECIFICATION OUTLINE

This valuable 16-page document is critical to building your house correctly. Designed to be filled in by you or your builder, this booklet lists 166 stages or items crucial to the building process.

For the layman, it provides a comprehensive review of the construction process and helps in making the specific choices of materials, models and processes. For the builder, it serves as a guide to preparing a building quotation and forms the basis for the construction program.

Designed primarily as a reference for the homeowner, this Specification Outline can become a legally binding document. Once it is filled out and agreed upon by owner and builder, it becomes a complete Project Specification.

When combined with the blueprints, a signed contract and schedule, the Specification Outline becomes a legal document and record for the building of your home. Many home builders find it useful to order two of these outlines—one as a worksheet in formulating the specifications and another to be carefully completed as a legal document.

DETAIL SHEETS

If you want to know more about techniques—and deal more confidently with subcontractors—we offer these remarkably useful detail sheets. Each is an excellent tool that will enhance your understanding of these technical subjects.

Plan-A-Home®

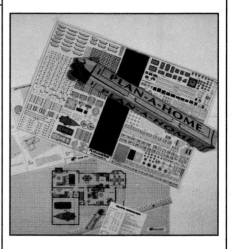

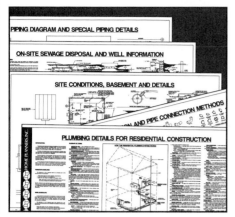

PLUMBING

The Blueprint Package includes locations for all the plumbing fixtures in your new house, including sinks, lavatories, tubs, showers, toilets, laundry trays and water heaters. However, if you want to know more about the complete plumbing system, these 24x36-inch detail sheets will prove very useful. Prepared to meet requirements of the National Plumbing Code, these six fact-filled sheets give general information on pipe schedules, fittings, sump-pump details, water-softener hookups, septic system details and much more. Color-coded sheets include a glossary of terms.

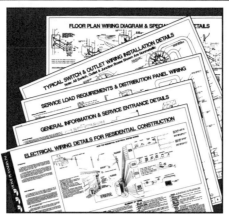

ELECTRICAL

The locations for every electrical switch, plug and outlet are shown in your Blueprint Package. However, these Electrical Details go further to take the mystery out of household electrical systems. Prepared to meet requirements of the National Electrical Code, these comprehensive 24x36-inch drawings come packed with helpful information, including wire sizing, switch-installation schematics, cable-routing details, appliance wattage, door-bell hookups, typical service panel circuitry and much more. Six sheets are bound together and color-coded for easy reference. A glossary of terms is also included.

Plan-A-Home® is an easy-to-use tool that helps you design a new home, arrange furniture in a new or existing home, or plan a remodeling project. Each package contains:

- More than *700 peel-off planning symbols* on a self-stick vinyl sheet, including walls, windows, doors, all types of furniture, kitchen components, bath fixtures and many more. All are made of durable, peel-and-stick vinyl you can use over and over.

- A reusable, transparent, *1/4-inch scale planning grid* made of tough mylar that matches the scale of actual working drawings (1/4 -inch equals 1 foot). This grid provides the basis for house layouts of up to 140x92 feet.

- *Tracing paper* and a protective sheet for copying or transferring your completed plan.

- A *felt-tip pen*, with water-soluble ink that wipes away quickly.

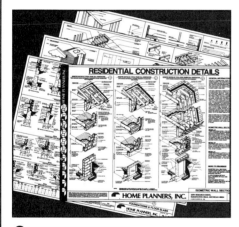

CONSTRUCTION

The Blueprint Package contains everything an experienced builder needs to construct a particular house. However, it doesn't show all the ways that houses can be built, nor does it explain alternate construction methods. To help you understand how your house will be built—and offer additional techniques—this set of drawings depicts the materials and methods used to build foundations, fireplaces, walls, floors and roofs. Where appropriate, the drawings show acceptable alternatives. These six sheets will answer questions for the advanced do-it-yourselfer or home planner.

MECHANICAL

This package contains fundamental principles and useful data that will help you make informed decisions and communicate with subcontractors about heating and cooling systems. The 24 x 36-inch drawings contain instructions and samples that allow you to make simple load calculations and preliminary sizing and costing analysis. Covered are today's most commonly used systems from heat pumps to solar fuel systems. The package is packed full of illustrations and diagrams to help you visualize components and how they relate to one another.

With Plan-A-Home®, you can make basic planning decisions for a new house or make modifications to an existing house. Use with your Blueprint Package to test modifications to rooms or to plan furniture arrangements before you build. Plan-A-Home® lets you lay out areas as large as a 7,500 square foot, six-bedroom, seven-bath house.

Home Plans Price Schedule & Index

These pages contain all the information you need to price your blueprints. In general, the larger and more complicated the house, the more it costs to design and thus the higher the price we must charge for the blueprints. Remember, however, that these prices are far less than you would normally pay for the services of a licensed architect or professional designer. Custom home designs and related architectural services often cost thousands of dollars, ranging from 5% to 15% of the cost of construction. By ordering our blueprints you are potentially saving enough money to afford a larger house, or to add those "extra" amenities such as a patio, deck, swimming pool or even an upgraded kitchen or luxurious master suite.

To use the index below, refer to the design number listed in chronological order (a helpful page reference is also given). Note the price index letter and refer to the House Blueprint Price Schedule at right for the cost of one, four or eight sets of blueprints or the cost of a reproducible sepia. Additional prices are shown for identical and reverse blueprint sets, as well as a very useful Materials List to accompany your plans.

House Blueprint Price Schedule
(Prices guaranteed through December 31, 1995)

	1-set Study Package	4-set Building Package	8-set Building Package	1-set Reproducible Sepias
Schedule A	$240	$300	$360	$460
Schedule B	$280	$340	$400	$520
Schedule C	$320	$380	$440	$580
Schedule D	$360	$420	$480	$640
Schedule E	$480	$540	$600	$700

Additional Identical Blueprints in same order................$50 per set
Reverse Blueprints (mirror image)....................$50 per set
Specification Outlines ....$10 each
Materials Lists:
      Schedule A-D $40
      Schedule E $50
Exchanges........$50 exchange fee for the first set; $10 for each
      additional set
      $70 total exchange fee for 4 set
      $100 total exchange fee for 8 set

Outdoor Amenities Index

Additional Sets for any of the above Outdoor Amenities are $10.00 each.

Toll Free 1-800-521-6797
Normal Office Hours:
    8:00 a.m. to 8:00 p.m.
    Eastern Time

When ordering by phone, please have your charge card ready. We'll also ask you for the Order Form Key Number on the opposite page. Please use our Toll-Free number for blueprint and book.

If we receive your order by 4:00 p.m. Eastern Time, we'll process it the same day and ship it the following day.

By FAX: Copy the Order Form on the next page and send it on our FAX line: 1-800-224-6699 or 1-602-297-9937.

Canadian Customers
Order Toll-Free 1-800-561-4169
For faster service and plans that are modified for building in Canada, customers may now call in orders directly to our Canadian supplier of plans and charge the purchase to a charge card. Or, you may complete the order form at right, adding 30% to all prices and mail in Canadian funds to:

The Plan Centre
20 Cedar Street North
Kitchener, Ontario N2H 2W8

By FAX: Copy the Order Form at right and send it via our Canadian FAX line: 1-519-743-1282.

BLUEPRINTS ARE NOT RETURNABLE

Before You Order . . .

Before completing the coupon at right or calling us on our Toll-Free Blueprint Hotline, you may be interested to learn more about our service and products. Here's some information you will find helpful.

Quick Turnaround
We process and ship every blueprint order from our office within 48 hours. Normally, if we receive your order by 4 p.m. Eastern Time, we'll process it the same day and ship it the following day. Because of the quick turnaround, we won't send a formal notice acknowledging receipt of your order.

Our Exchange Policy
Since blueprints are printed in response to your order, we cannot honor requests for refunds. However, we will exchange your entire first order for an equal number of blueprints plus the following exchange fees: $50 for the first set, $10 for each additional set; $70 total exchange fee for 4 sets: $100 total exchange fee for 8 sets. . . *plus* the difference in cost if exchanging for a design in a higher price bracket, or *less* the difference in cost if exchanging for a design in a lower price bracket. **(Sepias are not exchangeable.)** All sets from the order must be returned before the exchange can take place. Please add $10 for postage and handling via ground service; $20 via 2nd Day Air; $30 via Next Day Air.

About Reverse Blueprints
If you want to build in reverse of the plan as shown, we will include an extra set of reverse blueprints (mirror image) for an additional fee of $50. Although lettering and dimensions appear backward, reverses will be a useful visual aid if you decide to flop the plan.

Modifying or Customizing Our Plans
With over 2,500 different plans from which to choose, you are bound to find a Home Planners' design that suits your lifestyle, budget and building site. In addition, our plans can be customized to your taste by your choice of siding, decorative detail, trim, color and other non-structural alterations.

If you do need to make minor modifications to the plans, these can normally be accomplished by your builder without the need for expensive blueprint modifications. However, if you decide to revise the plans significantly, we strongly suggest that you order our reproducible sepias and consult a licensed architect or professional designer to help you redraw the plans to your particular needs.

Architectural and Engineering Seals
Some cities and states are now requiring that a licensed architect or engineer review and "seal" your blueprints prior to construction. This is often due to local or regional concerns over energy consumption, safety codes, seismic ratings, etc. For this reason, you may find it necessary to consult with a local professional to have your plans reviewed. This can normally be accomplished with minimum delays, for a nominal fee.

Compliance with Local Codes and Regulations
At the time of creation, our plans are drawn to specifications published by the Building Officials and Code Administrators (BOCA) International, Inc.; the Southern Building Code Congress (SBCCI) International, Inc.; the International Conference of Building Officials; or the Council of American Building Officials (CABO). Our plans are designed to meet or exceed national building standards. Some states, counties and municipalities have their own codes, zoning requirements and building regulations. Before building, contact your local building authorities to make sure you comply with local ordinances and codes, including obtaining any necessary permits or inspections as building progresses. In some cases, minor modifications to your plans by your builder, architect or designer may be required to meet local conditions and requirements. Home Planners may be able to make these changes to plans providing you supply all pertinent information from your local building authorities.

Foundation and Exterior Wall Changes
Most of our plans are drawn with either a full or partial basement foundation. Depending on your specific climate or regional building practices, you may wish to convert this basement to a slab or crawlspace. Most professional contractors and builders can easily adapt your plans to alternate foundation types. Likewise, most can easily change 2x4 wall construction to 2x6, or vice versa. If you need more guidance on these conversions, our handy Construction Detail Sheets, shown on page 109, describe how such conversions can be made.

How Many Blueprints Do You Need?
A single set of blueprints is sufficient to study a home in greater detail. However, if you are planning to obtain cost estimates from a contractor or subcontractors—or if you are planning to build immediately—you will need more sets. Because additional sets are cheaper when ordered in quantity with the original order, make sure you order enough blueprints to satisfy all requirements. The following checklist will help you determine how many you need:

_____ Owner

_____ Builder (generally requires at least three sets; one as a legal document, one to use during inspections, and at least one to give to subcontractors)

_____ Local Building Department (often requires two sets)

_____ Mortgage Lender (usually one set for a conventional loan; three sets for FHA or VA loans)

_____ TOTAL NUMBER OF SETS

HOUSE ORDER FORM

HOME PLANNERS, INC., 3275 WEST INA ROAD
SUITE 110, TUCSON, ARIZONA 85741

THE BASIC BLUEPRINT PACKAGE
Rush me the following (please refer to the Plans Index and Price Schedule in this section):

_____ Set(s) of blueprints for
plan number(s) _____. $_____

_____ Set(s) of sepias for
plan number(s) _____. $_____

_____ Additional identical blueprints in same
order @ $50 per set. $_____

_____ Reverse blueprints @ $50 per set. $_____

IMPORTANT EXTRAS
Rush me the following:

_____ Materials List: @ $40 Schedule A-D;
$50 Schedule E $_____

_____ Specification Outlines @ $10 each. $_____

_____ Detail Sets @ $14.95 each; any two for $22.95; any
three for $29.95; all four for $39.95 (save $19.85). $_____
❏ Plumbing ❏ Electrical ❏ Construction ❏ Mechanical
(These helpful details provide general construction
advice and are not specific to any single plan.)

_____ Plan-A-Home® @ $29.95 each. $_____

POSTAGE AND HANDLING	1-3 sets	4+ sets
DELIVERY (Requires street address - No P.O. Boxes)		
•Regular Service (Allow 4-6 days delivery)	❏ $8.00	❏ $10.00
•2nd Day Air (Allow 2-3 days delivery)	❏ $12.00	❏ $20.00
•Next Day Air (Allow 1 day delivery)	❏ $22.00	❏ $30.00
POST OFFICE DELIVERY	❏ $10.00	❏ $14.00
If no street address available. (Allow 4-6 days delivery)		
OVERSEAS DELIVERY Note: All delivery times are from date Blueprint Package is shipped.	fax, phone or mail for quote	

POSTAGE (From shaded box above) $_____
SUB-TOTAL $_____
SALES TAX (Arizona residents add 5% sales tax; Michigan residents add 6% sales tax.) $_____
TOTAL (Sub-total and tax) $_____

YOUR ADDRESS (please print)
Name _____

Street _____

City _____State_____Zip_____

Daytime telephone number (_____) _____

FOR CREDIT CARD ORDERS ONLY
Please fill in the information below:
Credit card number _____
Exp. Date: Month/Year _____
Check one ❏ Visa ❏ MasterCard ❏ Discover Card

Signature _____

Please check appropriate box: ❏ Licensed Builder-Contractor
❏ Homeowner

By FAX: Copy the order form above and sent it on our Fax Line: 1-800-224-6699 or 1-602-297-9937

 ORDER TOLL FREE
1-800-521-6797 or
602-297-8200

Order Form Key
TB19BP

1. ENCYCLOPEDIA OF HOME DESIGNS (EN) Our best collection of plans is now bigger and better than ever! Over 500 plans organized by architectural category. Includes all types and styles. The most comprehensive plan book ever. 352 pages. $9.95 ($12.95 Can.)

2. 200 BUDGET-SMART HOME PLANS (BS) The definitive source for the home builder with a limited budget—have your home and enjoy it too! Amenity-laden homes, in many sizes and styles, can all be built from our plans. 224 pages. $7.95 ($10.95 Can.)

3. ONE-STORY HOMES (V1) A collection of 470 homes to suit a range of budgets in one-story living. All popular styles, including Cape Cod, Southwestern, Tudor and French. 384 pages. $9.95 ($12.95 Can.)

4. TWO-STORY HOMES (V2) 478 plans for all budgets in a wealth of styles: Tudors, Salt-boxes, Farmhouses, Victorians, Georgians, Contemporaries and more. 416 pages. $9.95 ($12.95 Can.)

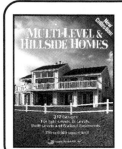

5. MULTI-LEVEL AND HILLSIDE HOMES (V3) 312 distinctive styles for both flat and sloping sites. Includes exposed lower level, open staircases, balconies, decks and terraces. 320 pages. $6.95 ($9.95 Can.)

6. VACATION AND SECOND HOMES (V4) 258 Ideal plans for a favorite vacation spot, perfect retirement or starter home. Includes cottages, chalets and one-, 1½-, two-story, and multi-level homes. 256 pages. $7.95 ($10.95 Can.)

7. THE HOME LANDSCAPER (HL) 55 fabulous front and back-yard plans that even the do-it-yourselfer can master. Complete construction blueprints and regionalized plant lists available for each design. 208 pages. $12.95 ($16.95 Can.)

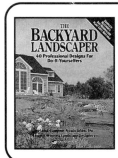

8. THE BACKYARD LANDSCAPER (BYL) Sequel to *The Home Landscaper*, contains 40 professionally designed plans for backyards. Do yourself or contract out. Complete construction blueprints and regionalized plant lists available. 160 pages. $12.95 ($16.95 Can.)

9. VICTORIAN DREAM HOMES (VDH) 160 Victorian and Farmhouse designs by three master designers. Victorian style from Second Empire homes through the Queen Anne and Folk Victorian era. Beautiful renderings with modern floor plans. 192 pages. $12.95 ($16.95 Can.)

Additional Books Order Form

To order your Home Planners books, just check the box of the book numbered below and complete the coupon. We will process your order and ship it from our office within 48 hours. Send coupon and check (in U.S. funds) to: Home Planners, Inc, 3275 W. Ina Rd., Ste.110, Dept. BK, Tucson, AZ 85741

YES! Please send me the design books I've indicated:

- ☐ **1: Encyclopedia of Home Designs (EN)** ....$ 9.95 ($12.95 Can.)
- ☐ **2: Budget-Smart Home Designs (BS)** ....$ 7.95 ($10.95 Can.)
- ☐ **3: One-Story Homes (V1)** ....$ 9.95 ($12.95 Can.)
- ☐ **4: Two-Story Homes (V2)** ....$ 9.95 ($12.95 Can.)
- ☐ **5: Multi-Level & Hillside Homes (V3)** ....$ 6.95 ($ 9.95 Can.)
- ☐ **6: Vacation & Second Homes (V4)** ....$ 7.95 ($10.95 Can.)
- ☐ **7: The Home Landscaper (HL)** ....$12.95 ($16.95 Can.)
- ☐ **8: The Backyard Landscaper (BYL)** ....$12.95 ($16.95 Can.)
- ☐ **9: Victorian Dream Homes (VDH)** ....$12.95 ($16.95 Can.)

CANADIAN CUSTOMERS: Order books toll-free: 1-800-561-4169. Or, complete this form, using Canadian prices and adding postage, and mail with Canadian funds to: The Plan Centre, 20 Cedar Street North, Kitchener, Ont. N2H 2W8.
FAX: 1-519-743-1282.

Home Planners, Inc.
3275 W Ina Road, Suite 110, Dept. BK, Tucson, AZ 85741

Additional Books Sub-Total $ _____
ADD Postage and Handling $ __3.00__
Ariz. residents add 5% Sales Tax; Mich. residents
add 6% Sales Tax $ _____
YOUR TOTAL (Sub-Total, Postage/Handling, Tax) $ _____

YOUR ADDRESS (Please print)

Name _____

Street _____

City _____ State _____ Zip _____

Phone (_____) _____ — _____

YOUR PAYMENT
Check one: ☐ Check   ☐ Visa   ☐ MasterCard   ☐ Discover Card
Required credit card information:

Credit Card Number _____

Expiration Date (Month/Year) _____ / _____

Signature Required _____

TO ORDER BOOKS BY PHONE
1-800-322-6797

TB19BK